'and some brought flowers'

'and some brought flowers'

Plants in a new world

Selected and introduced by
Mary Alice Downie and Mary Hamilton

Illustrations by E.J. Revell

Fitzhenry & Whiteside

'and some brought flowers'
Copyright © 2002 Fitzhenry & Whiteside

Fitzhenry and Whiteside Limited
195 Allstate Parkway
Markham, Ontario L3R 4T8

In the United States:
121 Harvard Avenue, Suite 2
Allston, Massachusetts 02134

www.fitzhenry.ca godwit@fitzhenry.ca

Fitzhenry & Whiteside acknowledges with thanks the Canada Council for the Arts, the Government of Canada through its Book Publishing Industry Development Program, and the Ontario Arts Council for their support of our publishing program.

National Library of Canada Cataloguing in Publication Data
Main entry under title:
 "And some brought flowers" : plants in a new world

Includes bibliographical references.
ISBN 1-55041-616-2

1. Botany—Canada—Pictorial works. 2. Botany—Canada—History. 3. Botany—Canada—Quotations, maxims, etc. I. Downie, Mary Alice, 1934- II. Hamilton, Mary, 1927- III. Revell, E. J. (Ernest John), 1934- IV. Title.

QK201.A539 2002   581.971 C2001-902815-6

U.S. Publisher Cataloging-in-Publication Data

"And some brought flowers" : plants in a new world / selected and introduced by Mary Alice Downie and Mary Hamilton ; illustrated by E.J. Revell.
Originally published: Toronto: University of Toronto, 1980.
Includes bibliographic references.
[176] p. : col. ill. ; cm.
Summary: An illustrated guide to North American plants. Includes overview, Latin names, growing regions, illustrations, and detailed descriptions by botanists and explorers.

ISBN 1-55041-616-2 (pbk.)

1. Botany—Canada. 2. Botany—Canada—History. 3. Botany—Canada—Quotations, maxims, etc. 4. Botanical illustration—Canada. I. Downie, Mary Alice, 1934- . II. Hamilton, Mary, 1927- . III. Revell, E. J. (Ernest John), 1934- . IV. Title.
582.13/0971 21   CIP   QK201.A54 2002

Cover design by Karen Petherick
Interior design by Antje Linger
Printed and bound in Canada

To JOHN DOWNIE, ALBERT CHARLES HAMILTON and ANN REVELL

ACKNOWLEDGMENTS

Nearly all the drawings for this book were made during the 1979 season. A few were done earlier; among these are pictures from the collections of Mr and Mrs Paul Adams and Mr and Mrs Ian MacGregor. I am most grateful to the owners for allowing me to use them.

With so many plants to paint in a relatively short time extensive travel was impossible, so that natives of western Canada had to be drawn from photographs (as camass and Indian potato), or represented by an eastern relative (as lupine and cactus). The other plants can be found in southern Ontario – an astonishing number even in the parks of Toronto. Even so, it was a formidable task to be in the right place at the right time to draw each particular plant. Undoubtedly many would have been missed if friends had not provided me with specimens, or told me where to find them. I am particularly grateful to Paul Catling, Margaret and John Catto, Emily Hamilton, Eleanor and Emerson Skelton, and Molly and Dick Ussher for help of this sort, but a full catalogue of names would include many I do not know, since one of the pleasures of doing the work was the fact that, whenever I asked, people were interested and helpful.   E.J.R.

We would like to thank our Technical Consultant, Dr Adèle Crowder, Curator of the Queen's Herbarium, who had the stamina to read an unwieldy manuscript several times and the knowledge to make many valuable contributions.

We are grateful to Dr R.S.G. Bidwell of Wallace, Nova Scotia, and John H. Hudson of Vanscoy, Sask. for their advice. We acknowledge the assistance of Dr Roy Taylor of the University of British Columbia, who kindly provided various plant specimens as did Mr Russell Ferguson, Period Gardener at Bellevue House, Kingston.

We also wish to thank William F.E. Morley of Special Collections, Douglas Library, Queen's University, who was, as always, extremely helpful; Helen M. Cobb who located several elusive volumes; and Mrs Shirlee Anne Smith, Archivist of the Hudson's Bay Company Archives in Winnipeg, Manitoba; and Jane Graham and Paulette Chiasson of the DCB staff who solved various biographical mysteries.

We owe a particular debt of gratitude to Prudence Tracy, for her immediate response to the manuscript, her sustained interest and perceptive guidance; and to our families for their patience. M.A.D. / M.H.

CONTENTS

ILLUSTRATIONS

INTRODUCTION

When Martin Frobisher reached the coast of Labrador in 1576 he found the prospect forbidding. There was, he tells us, 'so great store of ice all the coast along, so thick together, that hardly his boat could pass unto the shore. At length, after divers attempts, he commanded his company, if by any possible means they could get ashore, to bring him whatsoever thing they could first find, whether it were living or dead, stock or stone, in token of Christian possession … and some brought flowers …'

The token that fired Frobisher's imagination was a glittering stone, which conjured up visions of great mineral wealth. Yet, in many ways the flowers brought back were the true symbol of the country's wealth. Plants and trees were to provide settlers with food, shelter, medicine, transportation, and such necessary incidentals as dyes, barrel staves, baskets, and roofing material. In this book we have used quotations from a variety of early travellers and settlers describing the plants they found in Canada. The material is organized alphabetically, in the tradition of the old herbals, and botanical descriptions accompany detailed illustrations of the plants. The quotations reflect the practical, aesthetic, and botanical interests of pioneers in different parts of the country. They also illustrate early responses to the land.

Those who came to Canada were constantly astonished by both its harshness and its bounty. This ambivalent response is vividly summed up by the explorer-artist, Lieutenant Hood, who is astonished when the melting snow reveals the already green leaves of strawberries, gooseberries, and roses. 'The gifts of nature,' he writes, 'are disregarded and undervalued till they are withdrawn, and in the hideous regions of the Arctic Zone, she would make a convert of him for whom the gardens of Europe had no charms, or the mild beauties of a southern clime had bloomed in vain.'

The visitors learned much about North American plants from the country's first Aboriginal inhabitants. Domagaya taught Cartier that 'Anedda' or white cedar would cure scurvy, the disease afflicting his crew. Indian guides often sustained explorers with baked acorns, reindeer moss, or the disagreeable but indispensable tripe de roche. In this way, for example, an Indian woman saved Alexander Henry's men when they were starving and near cannibalism during a journey to Sault Sainte-Marie:

> I ascended a lofty mountain, on the top of which I found a very high rock, and this covered with a lichen, which the Chipeways call *waac* … The woman was well

acquainted with the mode of preparing the lichen for the stomach, which is done by boiling it down into a mucilage, as thick as the white of an egg. In a short time, we obtained a hearty meal; for though our food was of a bitter and disagreeable taste, we felt too much joy in finding it, and too much relief in eating it, not to partake of it with appetite and pleasure.

The quotations are interesting not only as a record of Native knowledge and of life in early Canada but also because they are part of an impressive scientific record. The distinguished botanist Frère Marie-Victorin writes that: 'the early history of Canadian Botany is pre-Linnean and goes back to the great epoch when Tournefort and his associates of the *Jardin des Plantes* of Paris were laying the foundation of modern systematic Botany.'

The first book on the subject was published in 1635 by Jacques Philippe Cornut, a Parisian physician, who had never been to Canada. The beautifully illustrated descriptions of North American plants in his *Canadensium Plantarum Historia* were probably taken from specimens in the Jardin des Plantes. For nearly a century this garden (earlier called the Jardin du Roi) was the most important in Europe. French explorers, settlers, and missionaries sent plants there to be cultivated for medical and botanical purposes. Thus Père Sagard writes early in the seventeenth century of the meadows beside the St Charles River: 'they are bespangled in summer with many small flowers particularly with what we call cardinals and matagon lilies, bearing a number of blossoms on one stock, nearly six, seven, or eight feet high; the savages eat the bulb, roasting it in the ashes, and it is quite good. We brought some to France, along with some cardinal plants, as rare flowers, but they did not succeed nor come to perfection as they do in their own climate and native soil.'

Louis Hébert, the first settler on the St Lawrence, was an 'apothicaire' which meant, in effect, a practical botanist. Canada's first professional botanist was Michel Sarrazin, 'un médecin du Roi.' He collected flora and fauna of the colony for the French botanist, Joseph de Tournefort, and produced, with the French botanist Sébastien Vaillant, a rare pre-Linnean manuscript, *L'Histoire des plantes de Canada*. His name is perpetuated in the pitcher plant *Sarracenia purpurea*. In 1744 the celebrated Jesuit scholar, Pierre de Charlevoix, used Sarrazin's text and many of the illustrations from Cornut's book for his own *Histoire et description générale de la Nouvelle-France*.

Another early name in Canadian botany is the Sieur de Dièreville, a surgeon who visited Acadia in 1699 and wrote an account of his voyage, partially in verse, with much information about the flora and fauna of that part of the country. He brought a number of plant specimens to Tournefort, who named *Diervilla* (Honeysuckle) in his honour.

In the mid-eighteenth century the Swedish naturalist Peter Kalm, who was a friend and protegé of Linneus, visited Quebec. There he met fellow-botanist Jean-François Gaulthier, another 'médecin du Roi,' after whom is named the common Wintergreen (*Gaultheria procumbens*). Kalm had been sent by the Swedish Academy of Sciences to observe the climate, soil, plants, animals, and people of North America. In his *Travels* he has left us an unparalleled view of colonial life.

But few Canadians had Kalm's botanical training and they learned through experience and observation. The story of ginseng, a root prized in China for more than five thousand years, is dramatic proof of this. According to Shen Nung's *Materia Medica* c AD 196 the root is: 'a tonic to the five viscera, quieting the spirits, establishing the soul, allaying fear, expelling evil effluvia, brightening the eye, opening the heart [and] benefiting the understanding.' In twelfth-century China it sold for its weight in silver because of its rarity. In the seventeenth and eighteenth centuries, the missionary Jesuits in China described the 'précieuse plante' in the Relations which they sent annually to Paris. In 1711 Père Pierre Jartoux speculates that, since the plant ranges in China in rugged forest areas between the thirty-ninth and forty-seventh degree of latitude north, 'this leads me to think that if ginseng is to be found in any other country in the world, it must chiefly be in Canada, where the forest and mountains – according to those who have lived there – are very much like those of Tartary.'

Père Joseph Lafitau, who was working among the Iroquois at Sault St Louis near Montreal, read these remarks. In a mémoire to His Royal Highness, the Duc d'Orléans, he writes: 'It was quite by chance that I began to find out about ginseng ... After spending three months searching for the plant without success, I found it ... when I was not thinking of it at all, near a house which I was having built. It was in fruit, and the bright red of the berries caught my eye.' He called out a botanist from Quebec: 'together, we combed the woods, and I let him have the pleasure of discovering the ginseng for himself. When he had collected several roots, we went back to the hut to check them in the book he had brought ... to our great joy we found that the description corresponded so exactly with the plant that there was no longer any room for doubt ...'

The best specimen was packed in spirits of wine and sent to Paris, where it was inspected and presented to the Prince Regent himself, before being placed in the care of the Professeur royal in the Jardin des Plantes. Once it had been verified, Aboriginals dug up all the ginseng they could find and sold it for a few pennies a pound. Canadian merchants then sold it to China at an enormous profit. Control of the trade was soon taken over by the Compagnie des Indes. Unfortunately, greed ruined this enterprise which in 1752 was worth twenty thousand pounds sterling. 'The Canadians,' writes George Heriot, 'eager suddenly to enrich themselves, reaped this plant in May, when it should not have been gathered until September, and dried it in ovens, when its moisture should have been gradually evaporated in the shade.' The Chinese rejected the shipment because of its poor quality and it was a hundred years before the profitable trade could be re-established.

By 1738 the English – perhaps hoping to find another 'ginseng' – began expressing an interest in northern vegetation as well as in the fur trade. The Governor and Committee of the Hudson's Bay Company directed Richard Norton at Prince of Wales' Fort and James Isham at York Fort to:

plant in Small Boxes, some roots of the Several sorts of Herbs, Plants and Shrubs, that are in Your parts, and ... save at a proper time, some of the Seeds, Berries, Cones or Kernels of all things growing in Your Country, And send the same by our Ship, And that the Surgeon do write us the Indian names thereof, And give us a Particular discription with their Qualities, and his observations.

Isham responded with *Observations and Notes* in which he describes scurvy grass, gooseberries, cranberries, and other wild fruits, and Indian tea ('wishakapucka' or Labrador tea) which he says 'intirely cur'd me, being Very much Efflicted with a Nervous Disorder.' His assistant Andrew Graham, who wrote a valuable study of northern plants which was much plagiarized, has only recently been recognized as 'the pioneer naturalist of the North.'

As the explorers and fur traders pushed westward they recorded unfamiliar plants. Alexander Henry credits the Indian potato with saving the men of Portage la Prairie from starvation. Surveyor Peter Fidler discovers the prickly pear cactus of southern Alberta. While travelling in the interior of British Columbia, David Thompson describes the complicated Indian method of making black moss cakes. Captain Cook, on the west coast, comments on 'Wild Garlick.'

A number of professional botanists shared the difficulties and dangers of the explorers' lives in early Canada. Naturalist John Richardson, who accompanied Franklin on his first and second arctic expeditions, described many northern plants, some of which were vitally important: 'Not being able to find any *tripe de roche*, we drank an infusion of the Labrador tea plant, (*ledum palustre*), and ate a few morsels of burnt leather for supper.' Thomas Drummond, a member of Franklin's second expedition, became separated from his guide while conducting an independent botanical survey and lived entirely alone for two winter months in the wilds of northern Alberta. Archibald Menzies, the naturalist who accompanied Captain Vancouver on the *Discovery* in 1790, managed, in the face of exceptional difficulties, to describe many new west coast plants, including the beautiful Menzies Arbutus or madrona. Some years later, on an expedition which involved severe injuries and shipwreck, David Douglas identified many new western species, including the great fir of British Columbia which bears his name. It is on the work of these four intrepid men – Richardson, Drummond, Menzies, and Douglas, that W.J. Hooker's magisterial *Flora Boreali Americana* of 1833 is chiefly based.

Frederick Pursh was another ill-starred botanist, pursuing his risky study in the new land. He is usually credited with writing the first flora of America north of Mexico (claims are also made for André Michaux and Jean Robin) and he planned to write a flora of Canada. However, his material was destroyed by fire and he died, destitute, shortly afterwards in Montreal. Francis Masson also died in Montreal, a disappointed man, although not before he had sent 24 new species to England, including *Trillium grandiflorum*.

But of all the early botanists, surely the unluckiest and most persevering was a Scottish gardener. John Goldie, who had been a pupil of Hooker in Glasgow's Botanic Gardens, arrived in Canada in 1817. After botanizing in the Halifax area, he went to Quebec, 'carrying with me all the roots and specimens that I had obtained, which, together with the produce of two weeks' researches in the neighbourhood of Quebec, I put on board a vessel which was bound for Greenock, but never heard of them afterwards.'

So it was to continue. He met Pursh in Montreal, collected specimens in the North-eastern States, 'and having accumulated as large a load as my back would carry, I took my journey to Philadelphia … having again entrusted my treasures to the deep, I had again … the disappointment of never obtaining any intelligence whatever of them.' A third collection was lost in a shipwreck on the St Lawrence but Goldie did finally manage to get a collection of his plants overseas. Despite these discouraging youthful experiences Goldie brought his family to Canada in 1844 and settled in Waterloo County, Ontario. He left an interesting *Journal* but, typically, his botanical notes went astray.

Clearly, hazards were great for the early naturalists, whether professional or amateur.

They often complain, not only of the ever-present dangers of drowning, freezing, or starving, but of almost impenetrable underbrush, insuperable mountains, and indescribable mosquitoes; yet through it all, they persevered in their observations.

As time passed and settlement increased, various gifted amateurs, most of them women, delighted in chronicling their novel surroundings and 'bush gardens.' Of these, the most observant was Catharine Parr Traill who, besides documenting the emigrants' life in several books, sent seeds to Kew Gardens and made many precise studies of plants. Her *Canadian Wild Flowers* was published in 1868 with paintings by her niece, Agnes Fitzgibbon.

Other notable amateurs were Lady Dalhousie, who collected and catalogued Canadian plants, and Mrs Simcoe who, while travelling with her husband, the lieutenant governor of Upper Canada, frequently described plant uses. The roots of the sarsaparilla, she writes 'look like gold thread. When steeped in brandy they make a fine aromatic tincture.' In the Maritimes, Juliana Horatia Ewing, briefly stationed in Fredericton with her soldier husband, waxes enthusiastic over the perils of picking trilliums.

And, of course, there is the redoubtable Susanna Moodie, sister of Catharine Parr Traill and author of the famous recipe for dandelion coffee 'as fine as the best Mocha.' Despite her cantankerous view of the settler's life, Mrs Moodie sometimes writes lyrically of flowers. Speaking in the person of an old hunter, she says

These are God's pictures ... Is it not strange that these beautiful things are hid away in the wilderness, where no eyes but the birds of the air, and the wild beasts of the wood, and the insects that live upon them, ever see them? Does God provide, for the pleasure of such creatures, these flowers? Is His benevolence gratified by the admiration of animals whom we have been taught to consider as having neither thought nor reflection? When I am alone in the forest, these thoughts puzzle me.

Whether poetical or practical, professional or amateur, the quotations in this book, taken together, justify Marie-Victorin's pride in 'the very old history of Botany in this new country, and the great effort contributed by a small and young nation scattered over an immense territory, to the knowledge of plant life in general and of plant life in Canada.'

The pages that follow are organized alphabetically by common plant name, and the complete list of plants included can be found on page ix. Using the common name often results in the grouping together of plants which belong to different families, for example, the various cranberries. We have used H.J. Scoggan's nomenclature, but the common names are generally those of Britton and Brown. The nomenclature of the first edition has been retained. Readers who wish to check modern synonyms are referred to the many new floras such as the *Ontario Plant List 1998* (ed. S.G. Newmaster et al.) or the incomplete *Flora of North America* (ed. N. Morin). Each entry is illustrated by some member of its family, and where the illustration is not of the first-mentioned plant, the identity is indicated in the text as appropriate. The quotations are arranged chronologically, and are identified by the author, a short title for the work quoted, and an approximate date of the quotation, or, where more appropriate, of the publication. Brief biographical information and details of the sources can be found in the section of biographies beginning on page 143 and arranged alphabetically.

'and some brought flowers'

Ash

Olive Family / Oleaceae

BLACK ASH / *Fraxinus nigra*
Also called Brown Ash; Hoop Ash; Swamp-,
Basket- or Water-ash; Frêne gras.
Distinguishing features stalkless leaflets, dark
brown winter buds, and soft scaly bark.
   Found in swamps and wet woods, New-
foundland to Manitoba and in the United
States. Flowers April to June, before leaves
appear. Used mostly for decorative purposes.
WHITE ASH / *Fraxinus americana* (illustrated)
is found growing in rich woods, Ontario to
Nova Scotia, Prince Edward Island, and south.

AS FOR THE ASH [*Fresne*], some very fine and straight ones are seen. They are used for making the Biscayan pike-staffs; one could make enough of them to supply all the armies of the King.
   Nicolas Denys / Description and Natural History 1672

THE INDIAN BASKETS are made from the wood of the black-ash, beaten with a wooden maul till the wood readily separates in rings of one year's growth from the other, and is as it were stripped off in ribbons from one to two inches in width the whole length of the piece. These ribbons, or stripes, are again subdivided to any thickness required, dyed of various colours, and put by for use.
   They use the bark of the hemlock pine to dye red, indigo for blue, and the inner bark of the root of the white-ash for yellow, which, when mixed with indigo, forms a good green. The baskets made of the wood of the black-ash are very light and pretty; the settlers' wives purchase them for cap-baskets, and the larger ones to keep their linen in: a coarser sort is used by the farmers for a variety of purposes; I have made many a one myself, and found them very serviceable.
   Samuel Strickland / Twenty-Seven Years in Canada West 1853

Aster

Composite Family / Compositae

A genus of not less than 250 species, most of which are abundant in North America. West coast species include *Aster conspicuus, Aster ericoides* var. *pansus*, and *Aster subspicatus*. Common in the mid-west is the Purple-stemmed Aster (*Aster puniceus*) and others.
COMMON BLUE WOOD ASTER / *Aster cordifolius* (illustrated)
Also called Bee-wood; Tongue; Heart-leaved Aster.
Distinguishing features leaves broadly heart-shaped, flower heads small but numerous, violet or blue, occasionally white.
   A typical wide-ranging aster found in open woods and thickets, Nova Scotia, Prince Edward Island to Manitoba, and south.

THE FLORA of the fall, comprising asters, golden rods and wild-everlastings were all out, encircling the pearly grey rocks which strewed the barren, and every bush was wreathed with lines and webs of little spiders, marked by the myriads of minute dew-drops with which they were strung. Gradually warmed by the rays of the sun when, overcoming the surrounding barrier of the forest, they poured over the whole face of the scene, the little barren sparkled like fairy-land, the morning resolving itself into one of those glorious days for which the fall of the year is noted.
   Campbell Hardy / Forest Life in Acadie 1869

Balm

Mint Family / Labiatae

BEE BALM / *Monarda didyma*
Also called Oswego-tea; Red or Fragrant Balm;
Horse or Mountain Mint; Indian's-plume.
Distinguishing feature showy tubular scarlet
florets extending from a terminal flower head.
　　Found in moist soil, especially along streams.
Native in eastern United States, a garden escape
in southern Ontario and southwestern Quebec.
July to September.
WILD BERGAMOT / *Monarda fistulosa*: as
above, but purplish flowers, dry locations.
Northern Alberta to central Manitoba and
southwestern Quebec, and south.

A SWEET PURPLE FLOWER, the roots of which, infused in brandy make a wholesome
cordial. It is called Oswego bitter.
　　Elizabeth Simcoe / Diary 1792–6

[THE RUBY-THROATED HUMMINGBIRD] is particularly fond of the deep crimson
flowers of the sweet-smelling Balm (*Monarda Kalmiana*), and will return to these after a
few moments, even if repeatedly alarmed away. Last year, in the month of September ...
a female humming-bird came, and began sucking the flowers. I immediately ran into the
house for my insect net, but found that the bird was gone when I returned: I stationed
myself, however, close by the balm flowers, holding the net up in a position for striking,
that there might be no occasion for any previous motion if it should re-appear. I
remained perfectly still, and presently the bird came again, hovering over the flowers,
and probing them with its tongue within two feet of me, without any sign of fear. I
dashed at it, and succeeded in capturing it. I carried it into the house, and held it in my
hand, admiring its delicacy and beauty. It would lie motionless in my hand, feigning
death, then suddenly dart off like an arrow towards the window, strike against the glass,
and fall, and lie motionless as before. I at length killed it, not without regret; and having
taken out the eyes and viscera, stuffed it with cotton, imbued with a solution of corrosive
sublimate, which preserved it pretty well.
　　P.H. Gosse / The Canadian Naturalist 1840

Basswood

Linden Family / Tiliaceae

BASSWOOD / *Tilia americana*
Also called American Linden; Whitewood; Bois
blanc; Lime-wood, Bee-wood, Monkey-nut-
tree; Yellow Bass-wood; Wickup; Daddy-nuts;
Spoon-wood; Whistle-wood.

Tilia americana is the only basswood usually
described in Canada.
Distinguishing features heart-shaped,
coarse-toothed leaves; yellow flowers in clusters; light brown fruit attached to a single wing.

Found in rich woods in the company of other
hardwoods, New Brunswick to Saskatchewan,
and south. Flowers June to July.

Basswood is light, soft, and straight-grained,
excellent for hand-carving, modelling, and
cabinet work.

THE FRENCH called the linden 'bois blanc' (white wood). The Indian women used its
bark in place of hemp for laces with which to sew up their shoes. They were busy during
the evenings sewing up their footwear with this material and I could have sworn that it
was a fine hemp cord they used. They take the bark, boil it in water for a long time, pound
it with a wooden club until it becomes soft, fibrous and like swingled hemp. They sat
twisting them on their thighs.
Peter Kalm / Travels into North America 1753–61

I SET ABOUT making a bedstead. To this end I got four short, upright, forked pieces,
upon which I placed poles across, tying them with strips of the bark of the bass tree, wove
in longwise and across, so as to make a tolerable substitute for a ticking, on which I might
lie before the fire high and dry; on this I placed a mattress of spruce boughs, and
altogether, with my buffalo skin for a covering, I rested comfortably. – The bass tree has
a remarkably tough, stringy bark, which rips easily from the trunk, and is so strong and
flexible, that it serves all common purposes of rope. The wood, at the same time, is
almost as soft as a cabbage-stalk, and very white.
Sir George Head / Forest Scenes and Incidents 1829

Bayberry

Wax-Myrtle Family / Myricaceae

BAYBERRY / *Myrica pensylvanica*
Also called Candleberry; Small Waxberry.
Distinguishing features a shrub with shiny oval
leaves; fruit bluish-white, very waxy.
   Found in dry or moist sandy soil, eastern
Quebec, St Pierre and Miquelon, New
Brunswick to southern Newfoundland, and
south. Flowers April and May.

I HAVE NO NEED to economize in wax, for this country [the NE coast] furnishes me
with abundance. The islands of the sea are bordered with wild laurel, which in autumn
bears berries closely resembling those of the juniper-tree. Large kettles are filled with
them and they are boiled in water; as the water boils, the green wax rises, and remains on
the surface of the water. From a minot of these berries can be obtained nearly four livres
of wax; it is very pure and very fine, but is neither soft nor pliable. After a few
experiments, I have found that by mixing with it equal quantities of tallow, – either beef,
mutton, or elk, – the mixture makes beautiful, solid, and very serviceable candles. From
twenty-four livres of wax, and as many of tallow, can be made two hundred tapers more
than a royal foot in length. Abundance of these laurels are found on the Islands, and on
the shore of the sea; one person alone could easily gather four minots of berries daily.
The berries hang in clusters from the branches of the shrub. I sent a branch of them to
Quebec, with a cake of wax, and it was pronounced excellent.
   Sébastien Rale / Jesuit Relations 1716–27

Bedstraw

Madder Family / Rubiaceae

NORTHERN BEDSTRAW / *Galium boreale*
Also called Sawayan; Dyers Lady's Bedstraw.
Distinguishing features white flowers in compound clusters; narrow leaves in whorls.

Found in rocky soil, Alaska, Yukon, Alberta to Nova Scotia. May to August.

Other species found through most of Canada and south. The illustration shows *Galium claytonii* growing over Wild Calla.

IT GROWS ONLY about four inches high, yielding a small narrow pointed leaf, something resembling rosemary. It has a fibrous root which branches horizontally in the ground. It dyes a beautiful red with the assistance of the Amiscuminick berry [crowberry] and poplar-ashes. There is another species of a yellow colour similar to the red kind, which dyes a beautiful yellow simply. The Mithco Sawyan (i.e. the Red Sawyan) is not capable to perform the dye simply, but requires the following composition and management.

Having provided a vessel with a close cover, and one quart of water English measure, they put into it $2\frac{3}{4}$ ounces of the root with half an ounce of the porcupine quills. Boil them over a slow fire until the liquor but just covers the contents; the quills have now received a red tincture. Secondly, they put the quills into three pints of liquor, the infusion of the Amiscuminick berries, keeping it gently boiling as before, till the liquor is about half exhausted or so low that you can take a quill out without injuring the hand. Your quills now have received a red vermilion colour. Lastly put in a pint of Amiscuminick liquor boiling hot with $\frac{3}{4}$ ounces of the poplar ashes, take the whole off the fire, and keep stirring until it cools so as a person may put a finger into it without pain. Then set it by for a day, or a night, that the liqour may be quite cool; and when you take out the quills they will have received a beautiful durable red.

Andrew Graham / Observations on Hudson's Bay 1767–91

Beech

Beech Family / Fagaceae

AMERICAN BEECH / *Fagus grandifolia*
Distinguishing features a large forest tree
bearing bur-enclosed triangular nuts. Smooth,
light grey bark, thin papery leaves.

Found in rich soil, Nova Scotia, Prince Edward Island to Ontario, and south. Nuts ripe
September to October.

Beechwood is hard and close-grained, useful
as fuel and for making furniture.

WATER-BEECH / *Carpinus caroliniana* does
not belong to the Beech Family but rather to the
Birch Family (Betulaceae). It is also called Bois
de fer, American Hornbeam, Blue Beech, and
Ironwood. It is a small tree, found in moist
woods and along streams, southwestern
Quebec to Ontario, and south.

BEECHES [*Haistres*] occur there, which are large both in height and thickness; from
them can be made galley oars of forty and fifty feet in length, and others for the
fishermen [of Acadia], who need a good many, which they are obliged to bring from
France. One could make of them fine and good planking for the bottoms of ships, which
would be as good as the Oak; for it does not rot in the water, and it is no less strong, nor so
subject to splitting and to cracks, something which happens often with Oaks, and causes
leaks difficult to stop well.

Nicolas Denys / Description and Natural History 1672

HERE IS an abundance of beech trees in the woods, and they now have ripe seeds. The
people in Canada collect them in autumn, dry them and keep them till winter, when they
eat them instead of walnuts and hazel nuts; and I am told they taste very good …

The French call the water-beech (Carpinus) bois dur. They know of no other use for
the wood than that it is good for fuel, and since it is hard and durable, it is used for cart
axles.

Peter Kalm / Travels into North America 1753–61

Birch

Birch Family / Betulaceae

The Birch Family contains trees and shrubs found mostly in the northern hemisphere but also in South America. Arboreal species of birch occur across Canada and dwarf birches are amongst the hardier Arctic plants. *Betula papyrifera* (illustrated) is useful in diverse ways while *Betula lenta* provides good timber.

PAPER-BIRCH / *Betula papyrifera*
Also called White Birch; Canoe Birch; Silver Birch.
Distinguishing features a medium-sized tree with creamy-coloured papery bark and a somewhat shallow root system; flowers are unisexual catkins.

IT IS FOR their very curious bark-work that the sisters of this convent [the Ursulines at Trois-Rivières] are particularly distinguished. The bark of the birch tree is what they use, and with it they make pocket-books, work-baskets, dressing-boxes, &c.&c. which they embroider with elk hair, died of the most brilliant colours. They also make models of the Indian canoes, and various war-like implements used by the Indians.

Nearly all the birch bark canoes in use on the St. Lawrence and Utawa Rivers, and on the nearer lakes, are manufactured at Three Rivers, and in the neighbourhood, by Indians.

Isaac Weld / Travels through North America 1799

WANDERING NATIONS, such as the Algonquins, who remain but for a short time in one situation, are satisfied with making their huts extremely low, and with placing them in a confused manner. They generally carry with them large rolls of the bark of the birch-tree, and form the frames of the cabins of wattles or twigs stuck into the earth in a circular figure, and united near their upper extremities. Upon the outside of this frame the bark is unrolled, and thus affords shelter from rain and from the influence of the sun.

George Heriot / Travels through the Canadas 1807

IF YOU WANT any extra light [the Indians] make a candle in a moment with a twisted piece of birch bark, & if you desire to have it *fixed* it is set in a split stick planted in the ground; but it requires frequent snuffing. So if you are short at any time of a cup for drinking, or a vessel for bailing the canoe, the want is supplied in half a moment by a kind of bowl or scuttle of bark which if held properly, so as to keep it tight, in the hand, retains the water even without being stitched.

Bishop George Mountain / Visit to the Gaspé Coast 1824–6

NOT ONLY ARE THE CANOES in which the Indians trust themselves on lakes sufficiently boisterous, some miles from the shore, made of it, but also all sorts of small cups and dishes. Besides, it burns like pitch; splits into threads which serve for twine; and the filmy part, near the outside, may be written upon in pencil, making no bad substitute for paper.

Sir George Head / Forest Scenes and Incidents 1829

THE SQUAWS have a curious method of forming patterns upon this bark with their teeth, producing very elegant and elaborate designs. They double a strip of bark many times into angles, which they bite at the sharp corners in various forms. Upon the piece being unfolded, the pattern appears, which is generally filled in very ingeniously with beads and coloured porcupine quills. The squaws perform this work in the dark quite as well as in the daylight.

Samuel Strickland / Twenty-Seven Years in Canada West 1853

Bittersweet

Staff-Tree Family / Celastraceae

CLIMBING BITTERSWEET / *Celastrus scandens*
Also called Shrubby Bittersweet; Waxwork;
Staff-tree; Fever-twig; Climbing Orange-tree;
Jacob's-ladder; Bourreau des arbres.
Distinguishing features showy orange fruits
enclosing fleshy seeds on a twining vine.
   Found growing on trees, fences, or trailing
on the ground. Quebec to southeastern Saskatchewan, and south. Flowers in June.
   Climbing or Bitter Nightshade / *Solanum
dulcamara* is also called Bittersweet. An introduced species originating in Eurasia, it is
poisonous.

GOOD GOD! have mercy on so many poor innocent people … Those that have any life
seeketh out for roots, which could not be done without great difficulty, the earth being
frozen two or three foot deep, and the snow five or six above it. The greatest subsistence
that we can have is of rind tree, which grows like ivy about the trees. To swallow it, we
cut the stick some two foot long, tying it in [a] fagot, and boil it, and when it boils one
hour or two the rind or skin come off with ease, which we take and dry it in the smoke,
and then reduce it into powder betwixt two grain stones, and putting the kettle with the
same water upon the fire, we make it a kind of broth, which nourished us. But [we]
became thirstier and drier than the wood we eat. The first week we did eat our dogs.
   Pierre-Esprit Radisson / Explorations 1659–61

MARCH 11, 1801: There is also an abundance of bois tors [twisted wood], a short shrub
that winds up the stocks of larger trees; the wood is soft and spongy, with a thick bark,
which is often eaten by the natives in time of famine. There are two species of this shrub;
one grows much thicker than the other, and is very sweet, but too astringent. The
smaller kind is more insipid and less unwholesome. They cut it into pieces and boil it a
long time, when the bark is peeled off and eaten without any further preparation. I have
subsisted upon this bark for days, but always found my weakness increased upon me.
   Alexander Henry, the Younger / Journals 1799–1814

Bloodroot

Poppy Family / Papaveraceae

BLOODROOT / *Sanguinaria canadensis*
Also called Puccoon-root; Sang-dragon; Tet-
terwort; Red Indian-paint; Turmeric; Redroot;
Corn-root; Pauson; Sweet-slumber; White
Puccoon; Snake-bite.
Distinguishing features a showy delicate flower
with eight or more petals. The underground
stem exudes orange-coloured juice when
broken.
   Found in rich, rocky open woodland. Nova
Scotia to southeastern Manitoba and eastern
United States. Flowers April to May.

IN THE AFTERNOON we entered a lake [Lac des Chênes] five leagues long and two wide,
where there are very beautiful islands filled with vines, walnuts and other fine trees; and
10 or 12 leagues from there, up the river, we passed several islands covered with pines.
The soil is sandy, and a root is found there which makes a crimson dye, with which the
savages paint their faces and then they put on little gee-gaws in their own way.
   Samuel de Champlain / Voyages and Explorations 1604–16

THE BLOOD-ROOT, *sanguinaria* is worthy of attention from the root to the flower. As
soon as the sun of April has warmed the earth and loosened it from its frozen bonds, you
may distinguish a number of purely white buds, elevated on a naked footstalk, and
partially enfolded in a handsome vine-shaped leaf, of a pale bluish green, curiously
veined on the under side with pale orange. The leaf springs singly from a thick juicy
fibrous root, which, on being broken, emits a quantity of liquor from its pores of a bright
orange scarlet colour: this juice is used by the Indians as a dye, and also in the cure of
rheumatic and cutaneous complaints. The flowers of the *sanguinaria* resemble the white
crocus very closely.
   Catharine Parr Traill / The Backwoods of Canada 1836

Blueberry

Ericaceae

HUCKLEBERRY
Most of the family of the Ericaceae are trees and
shrubs, and many are dwarf shrubs which occur
in wet bogs or on heaths. The genus *Gaylus-
sacia* produces huckleberries, either black or
dark blue.

Vaccinium is a genus with many species including deerberry, bilberry, whortleberry, and
cowberry. The term blueberry is most generally used of the Early or Low-bush Blueberry /
Vaccinium angustifolium, also called Bluets,
Dwarf or Sugar Blueberry.

Found in dry, rocky or sandy soil, Newfoundland to Saskatchewan.

IT IS TRUE that God seems to have wanted to give to these frightful desert regions [the
section of the Ottawa River around Allumette Lake] something in its season to serve for
the refreshment of man and for the inhabitants of these places, for I assure you that there
are along the rivers a great quantity of blueberries, a small fruit very good to eat, and a
great many raspberries and other small fruits, and in such quantities that it is wonderful.
These fruits the inhabitants dry for their winter, as we do prunes in France for Lent.
  Samuel de Champlain / Voyages and Explorations 1604–16

SOME OF THEM [Indians] imagine a Paradise abounding in blueberries; these are little
blue fruits, the berries of which are as large as the largest grapes. I have not seen any of
them in France. They have a tolerably good flavor, and for this reason the souls like them
very much.
  Paul Le Jeune / Jesuit Relations 1639

THESE BERRIES serve for several uses, after they are dry'd in the Sun, or in an Oven; for
then they make Confits of 'em, or put 'em into Pyes, or infuse 'em in Brandy. The
North-Country Savages make a Crop of 'em in the Summer, which affords 'em very
seasonable relief, especially when their hunting comes short.
  Baron de Lahontan / New Voyages to North-America 1703

THE CEREMONY of adoption is as follows: – A feast is prepared of dog's flesh boiled in
bear's grease, with huckle berries, of which it is expected every one should heartily
partake. When the repast is over, the war song is sung ...
  John Long / Voyages and Travels 1791

[THEY ARE] larger than in England, quite black, and if dried in the sun make as good
puddings as Levant currants, quite as sharp. The Indians live in the woods where they
grow at this season of the year, and boil quantities of them into cakes.
  Elizabeth Simcoe / Diary 1792–6

Camass

Lily Family / Liliaceae

WESTERN CAMASS / *Camassia quamash*
Also called Common Camass; Early Camass;
Quamash; Wild Hyacinth; Swamp Sego.
Distinguishing features blue to dark blue
flowers growing abundantly in wet meadows.
The edible bulbs are found at a depth of two to
six inches. The Western Great Camass /
Camassia leichtlinii is similar; its bulbs are
about one inch in diameter and over two inches
long. Both varieties grow in southern British
Columbia and bloom May to June.

West Coast Indians reportedly fought over
flatlands where millions of dazzling blue camass
grew. They weeded out the bulbs of the
white-flowered Death Camass / *Zigadenus
venenosus*.

Eastern Camass / *Camassia scilloides*, is
found in southern Ontario, and south.

[THE INDIAN CHIEF] made a present of two half-dried salmon, and about half a bushel
of roots of two kinds: the one called *Ka-mass* a white root of a slight bitter taste which
becomes a favourite, and is agreeable to the stomach; the other is a kind of small onion,
which is dug out of the ground near the surface ... [They are] then washed and baked in a
smothered heat, when from white they become of a rich dark brown and very sweet.
They are nourishing, but eaten too freely without moss bread are apt to loosen the
bowels, and these two served for the rough bread and cheese of the country ...
David Thompson / Travels in Western North America 1784–1812

THEY ARE FOUND in immense quantities in the plains in the vicinity of Fort Vancouver,
and in the spring of the year present a most curious and beautiful appearance, the whole
surface presenting an uninterrupted sheet of bright ultra-marine blue, from the innu-
merable blossoms of these plants.

FORT VICTORIA stands upon the banks of an inlet in the island about seven miles long
and a quarter of a mile wide ... Its Indian name is the Esquimelt, or Place for gathering
Camas, great quantities of that vegetable being found in the neighbourhood.
Paul Kane / Wanderings of an Artist 1859 (both passages)

Cardinal Flower

Lobelia Family / Lobeliaceae

CARDINAL FLOWER / *Lobelia cardinalis*
Also called Red Lobelia; Red Betty; Slink-
weed; Hog's-physic.
Distinguishing features a loosely set spike of
velvety scarlet flowers; alternating lance-
shaped leaves.

Found in moist ground, New Brunswick to
Ontario, possibly southern Saskatchewan, and
south. July to September. A favourite of the
Ruby-throated Hummingbird.

Named for its similarity to the cap worn by
Roman Catholic cardinals.

Lobelia dortmanna and *Lobelia kalmii* are
found in the western United States and Canada
as well as in the east. Flowers are blue or laven-
der, fading to white.

IT IS IN our little river [the St Charles] that the savages catch an immense number of
eels in the autumn, and the French kill the game-birds which come to it in quantity. The
little meadows which border it are bespangled in summer with many small flowers,
particularly with what we call cardinals, and matagon lilies, bearing a number of
blossoms on one stalk, nearly six, seven, or eight feet high; the savages eat the bulb,
roasting it in ashes, and it is quite good. We brought some to France, along with some
cardinal plants, as rare flowers, but they did not succeed nor come to perfection as they do
in their own climate and native soil.

Gabriel Sagard / The Long Journey to the Country of the Hurons 1632

AT THE HEAD of the Katchawanook, the lake [Stony Lake] is divided by a long neck of
land that forms a small bay on the right-hand side, and a very brisk rapid on the left. The
banks are formed of large masses of limestone: and the cardinal-flower and the tiger-lily
seem to have taken an especial fancy to this spot, and to vie with each other in the display
of their gorgeous colours.

Susanna Moodie / Roughing it in the Bush 1852

Cedar

Pinaceae

No true cedars are native to North America. Our cedars are a species of either arbor-vitae or juniper. Two native North American species of arbor-vitae are found in Canada.

WHITE CEDAR / *Thuja occidentalis* (white arbor-vitae) (illustrated) is usually a small conical tree but it sometimes grows to a height of eighty feet. Prince Edward Island, Nova Scotia to Manitoba, north to Hudson Bay, and south.

The wood is the lightest in weight of Canadian timbers, but durable; excellent for canoes, posts, shingles, etc.

WESTERN RED CEDAR / *Thuja plicata* (giant arbor-vitae) is one of the largest trees in the Pacific region.

The Eastern Red Cedar is a species of Juniper, *Juniperus virginiana*. It is conical and shrub-like and has blue berry-like fruit.

OUR CAPTAINE considering our estate and how that sicknesse [scurvy] was encreased and hot amongst us, one day ... asked Domagaia how he had done to heale himselfe: he answered, that he had taken the juice and sappe of the leaves of a certain Tree, and therewith had healed himselfe ... two women ... shewed the way how to use it, and that is thus, to take the barke and leaves of the sayd tree, and boile them togither, then to drinke of the sayd decoction every other day, and to put the dregs of it upon his legs that is sicke ...

Our Captaine presently caused some of that drink to be made for his men to drink of it, but there was none durst tast of it, except one or two, who ventured the drinking of it, only to tast and prove it: the other seeing that did the like, and presently recovered their health, and were delivered of that sickenes, and what other disease soever ...

... a tree as big as any Oake in France was spoiled and lopped bare, and occupied all in five or six daies, and it wrought so wel, that if al the phisicians of Mountpelier and Lovaine had bene there with all the drugs of Alexandria, they would not have done so much in one yere, as that tree did in six dayes.

Jacques Cartier / Voyages 1535–6

WE SAW beautiful red cedars, the first that I had seen in this country, from which I made a cross, which I set up at one end of the island on a high place, well in sight, with the arms of France, as I have done in other places where we have stopped. I named this island St. Croix.

Samuel de Champlain / Voyages and Explorations 1604–16

I CANNOT BETTER express the fashion of the Huron dwellings than to compare them to bowers or garden arbors, – some ... are covered with cedar bark, [and] they are almost as susceptible to fire as matches.

Jean de Brébeuf / Jesuit Relations 1634–6

ABOUT HALF A MILE from hence [Niagara Falls, Table Rock], ... is placed the Indian ladder, composed of a tall cedar tree, whose boughs have been lopped off to within three inches of the trunk, and whose upper end is attached by a cord of bark to the root of a living tree; the lower end is planted amid stones. It is upwards of forty feet in length, and trembles and bends under the weight of a person upon it.

George Heriot / Travels through the Canadas 1807

Cherry

Rose Family / Rosaceae

WILD RED CHERRY / *Prunus pensylvanica*
Also called Pin Cherry; Pigeon Cherry; Bird-,
Red-, or Fire-cherry; Dogwood.
  This small tree has lance-shaped leaves and
clusters of white flowers. Found in sunny
locations, Newfoundland to British Columbia
and south. Flowers April to June. Fruit ripe
in August.
  Wild Black Cherry (*Prunus serotina*) is
similar.
CHOKE CHERRY / *Prunus virginiana*
There are several varieties which grow only in
western regions. The Red-fruited Choke
Cherry grows in both eastern and western
Canada and south.

AND NOW will give acco! of that same Country soile
Which hither part is very thick of wood
Affords small nutts wth little cherryes very good
Thus it continues till you leave ye woods behind
And then you have beast of several kind
The one is a black a Buffillo great
Another is an outgrown Bear ...
  Henry Kelsey / Journals 1690–2

THE CHERRIES are small, and extream red; and though their taste is not good, yet the
Roe-bucks like 'em so well, that in the Summer time they scarce ever miss to lye under
the Cherry-trees all Night long, especially if it blows hard.
  Baron de Lahontan / New Voyages to North-America 1703

THE TAWQUOY-MEEN-AHTICK of the Crees is a handsome small tree, rising on the
sandy plains of the Saskatchewan to the height of twenty feet, but extending as far north
as Great Slave Lake, where it attains the height of five feet only. Its fruit, termed
Tawquoy-meena, or Choke-cherry, is not very edible in a recent state, but when dried
and bruised, forms an esteemed addition to pemmican.
  John Richardson / Franklin: Narrative of a Journey 1823

THE BLACK CHERRY is, in its wild state, crude and astringent; it is used medicinally in
the United States for consumptive complaints; the value of the tree in Canada arises from
the beauty of the wood, which makes it prized for furniture.
  Samuel Strickland / Twenty-Seven Years in Canada West 1853

Clover

Pea Family / Leguminosae

There are about 275 species, most of them abundant in the north temperate zone. Three of the commonest are mentioned by Sir Richard Bonnycastle. All are thought to be introduced.
RABBIT'S-FOOT CLOVER / *Trifolium arvense*
Also called Old-field or Stone Clover; Hare's-foot- or Pussy-clover; Calf-clover; Poverty-grass; Bottle-grass; Dogsandcats; Pussies.

This clover has fuzzy oblong pinkish flowers. Found in fields and waste places, Vancouver Island, Quebec, Ontario, Prince Edward Island, Nova Scotia, and south. Flowers May to September.

RED, PURPLE, or MEADOW CLOVER / *Trifolium pratense* (illustrated)
Also called Honeysuckle-clover; Knap; Suckles; Marl- or Cow-grass; Broad-leaved Clover; Sugar-plums.

The familiar large-headed clover with pink or magenta flowers. Found almost throughout Canada and the United States.
WHITE CLOVER / *Trifolium repens*
Also called Dutch or Honeysuckle Clover; White Trefoil; Purple-grass; Purplewort; Sheep's Gowan; Honeystalks; Lamb-sucklings; Shamrocks.

The familiar white or pink-tinged clover found almost throughout Canada and the United States.

NATURAL CLOVER, trifolium arvense, pratense, and repens, the field, the red, and the white kinds, are common, and the vetch (vicia), both in Newfoundland and on the Labrador shore, covers the sandy banks near the sea to such an extent, that vessels on the latter coast requiring fodder, send their boats ashore to gather this rich natural crop; and sheep, in the neighbourhood of St. John's, are turned loose to a desert place near the Cape Spear Lighthouse, to fatten on it.

Sir Richard Henry Bonnycastle / Newfoundland in 1842

THE SOIL of this locality [Fort Victoria] is good, and wheat is grown in considerable abundance. Clover grows plentifully, and is supposed to have sprung from accidental seeds which had fallen from the packages of goods brought from England; many of which are made up in hay.

Paul Kane / Wanderings of an Artist 1859

Columbine

Crowfoot Family / Ranunculaceae

WILD COLUMBINE / *Aquilegia canadensis*
Also called Glands or Gants de Notre-Dame;
Rock-bells; Honeysuckle; Rock-lily;
Meeting-houses; Jack-in-trousers; Cluckies.
Distinguishing features a slender, branching
stem; scarlet, nodding flowers, the spurs nearly
straight. Found in rocky woods, eastern Saskatchewan to Newfoundland and Nova Scotia
(not known from Prince Edward Island), and
south. Flowers April to July.

Western species include the Blue Columbine / *Aquilegia brevistyla* and the Yellow
Columbine / *Aquilegia flavescens*.

'Aquilegia' from the Latin for eagle, referring to the fancied likeness of the spurs to
eagles' claws.

In the Language of Flowers, which flourished
in Victorian times, the Canadian Columbine
represented Folly, from its resemblance to the
jester's cap and bells.

THE ISLAND on which we breakfasted [on the return from Manitoulin] was in great part
white marble; and in the clefts and hollows grew quantities of gooseberries and raspberries, wild-roses, the crimson columbine, a large species of harebell, a sort of willow,
juniper birch, and stunted pine, and such was the usual vegetation.
Anna Jameson / Winter Studies and Summer Rambles 1838

THE WILD COLUMBINE is perennial and very easily cultivated. Its blossoms are eagerly
sought out by the bees and humming birds. On sunny days you may be sure to see the
latter hovering over the bright drooping bells, extracting the rich nectar with which they
are so bountifully supplied. Those who care for bees, and love humming birds, should
plant the graceful red-flowered Columbine in their garden borders.
Catharine Parr Traill / Canadian Wild Flowers 1868

Corn

Grass Family / Gramineae

INDIAN CORN or MAIZE / *Zea mays*
The most widely grown kind of maize is Field or Dent corn which is used for silage or grain. Other types, such as Sweet Corn and Popcorn, are used as food for man.

Indian corn, indigenous to America, was seen by Columbus in the West Indies. Champlain was the first to leave a record of its cultivation in New England.

[THE INDIANS] till and cultivate the soil, something which we have not hitherto observed. In the place of ploughs, they use an instrument of very hard wood, shaped like a spade. This river [coast of the Almouchiquois around Richmond Island] is called by the inhabitants of the country Chouacoet.

The next day Sieur de Monts and I landed to observe their tillage on the bank of the river. We saw their Indian corn, which they raise in gardens. Planting three or four kernels in one place, they then heap up about it a quantity of earth with shells of the signoc [horse-shoe crab] before mentioned. Then three feet distant they plant as much more, and thus in succession. With this corn they put in each hill three or four Brazilian beans, which are of different colours. When they grow up, they interlace with the corn, which reaches to the height of from five to six feet; and they keep the ground very free from weeds. We saw there many squashes, and pumpkins, and tobacco, which they likewise cultivate.

The Indian corn which we saw was at that time about two feet high, some of it as high as three. The beans were beginning to flower, as also the pumpkins and squashes.
Samuel de Champlain / Voyages 1604–8

WHEN THE MAIZE is in the ear and still green, some roast it on the coals, in which way it has an excellent flavour. They commonly regale strangers with this dish. They also send it in some places to persons of distinction who arrive in their village, much in the same manner as they present the freedom of a city in France.
Pierre-François-Xavier de Charlevoix / Journal of a Voyage 1744

When the time of harvest arrives, the women pluck with the hand the Indian corn, tie it by its leaves in bunches, and suspend it to be dried by the sun. It is afterwards stored in pits dug in the sides of a declivity, and lined with mats. It is thus preserved uninjured by moisture, and from being consumed by vermin. This constitutes a material part of the food of many of the northern sedentary tribes. A further office of the women is to grind the corn when dried, into a coarse flour, by means of stones, or of wooden utensils; and to fan it, that it may be freed from particles of chaff. When boiled, and mixed with grease or similar substances, it is called *sagamité*. A quantity of this food is every morning prepared for breakfast of the families.
George Heriot / Travels through the Canadas 1807

[A POOR IRISH SETTLER] had procured some whiskey from her next-door neighbour – some five or six miles off; and there it stood somewhat ostentatiously on the table in a 'greybeard,' with a 'corn cob', or ear of Indian corn stripped of its grain, for a cork.
Susanna Moodie / Roughing it in the Bush 1852

Cranberry

Honeysuckle Family / Caprifoliaceae

HIGH-BUSH CRANBERRY / *Viburnum opulus*
(illustrated)
Also called Cranberry-tree; Wild Guelder-
rose; Rose-elder; White Dogwood; Cherry-
wood; May-rose; Pincushion-tree.
Distinguishing features a high-growing shrub
with white flower clusters and maple-like
leaves; fruit spherical, translucent, red, and
very acid.
   Found in low ground, Newfoundland to
British Columbia. Flowers June to July.

Heath Family / Ericaceae

BOG, LARGE, OR AMERICAN CRANBERRY /
Oxycoccus macrocarpus
Also called Bear-berry; Marsh-cranberry.
Distinguishing features thread-like stems,
leaves ovate and evergreen; tiny pink flowers.
   Found in bogs, Newfoundland to Ontario,
possibly Manitoba and in the United States.
Fruit ripe September to October. This is the
species which is cultivated.
   The Small or European Cranberry /
Oxycoccus oxycoccus is similar and ranges
from Newfoundland to British Columbia.

WE HAVE FASTED many times ... once, while at She-than-nee, near seven days, during
which we tasted not a mouthful of any thing, except a few cranberries, water, scraps of
old leather, and burnt bones.

CRANBERRIES grow in great abundance near Churchill, and are not confined to any
particular situation, for they are as common on open bleak plains and high rocks as
among the woods. When carefully gathered in the Fall, in dry weather, and as carefully
packed in casks of moist sugar, they will keep for years, and are annually sent to England
in considerable quantities as presents, where they are much esteemed. When the ships
have remained in the Bay so late that the Cranberries are ripe, some of the Captains have
carried them home in water with great success.
   Samuel Hearne / A Journey from Prince of Wales's Fort 1795 (both passages)

THE INDIANS bring us cranberries in spring and autumn which are as large as cherries
and as good; the best grow under water.
   Elizabeth Simcoe / Diary 1792–6

A LARGE BEAR at the end of the fall will weigh five or even six hundred pounds; this has
been increased in domesticated specimens by oatmeal feeding to over seven hundred.
   Having awoke at last, the genial warmth of a spring day tempts him forth to try and
find something to appease the growing cravings of appetite. What is the bill of fare?
meagre enough generally, for the snow still covers the dead timber (where he might find
colonies of ants), the roots, and young shoots and buds; but he bethinks himself of the
cranberries in the open bogs from which, unshaded by the branches of the dark fir-forest,
the snow has disappeared, disclosing the bright crimson berries still clinging to their
tendrils on the moss-clumps and rendered tender and luscious by the winter's frost.
   Campbell Hardy / Forest Life in Acadie 1869

Dandelion

Composite Family / Compositae

COMMON DANDELION / *Taraxacum officinale*
Also called Blowball; Arnica; Lion's-tooth; Cankerwort; Milkwitch; Irish Daisy; Monk's-head; Priest's-crown; Puff-ball.
Distinguishing features the outer bracts which surround the inflorescence are bent sharply backward in this species.

Found in fields, waste places, and lawns throughout North America. Naturalized from Europe.
'Leontodon' from the Greek for lion's-tooth.
The Dwarf Dandelion mentioned by Bonnycastle is usually identified as *Krigia biflora*, a small species found in southeastern Manitoba, Ontario, and south.

BURRAGE, SORREL, and Coltsfoot, may be ranked among the useful plants. Dandelion is also plentiful at Churchill, and makes an early salad, long before any thing can be produced in the gardens.

In fact, notwithstanding the length of the Winter ... I never had one man under me who had the least symptoms of the scurvy.

Samuel Hearne / A Journey from Prince of Wales's Fort 1795

CHARLES – What is the origin of the name, dandelion?
F. – The word was originally *Dent-de-Lion*, that is, lion's tooth, the leaves being cut into curved teeth, pointing backward. The generic name signifies the same thing; this form of the leaf is called *runcinate*. In Newfoundland, the leaves of the dandelion are much sought after in spring, as a culinary vegetable; their taste, when boiled, is peculiar, but agreeable to many persons, and as this is the first eatable vegetable that appears, the meadows and fields are frequented at this season by boys and girls, who in cutting up the plant with knives, cut up a great deal of the grass also, and do considerable mischief. Here [in Quebec] it is not eaten.

P.H. Gosse / The Canadian Naturalist 1840

The dwarf dandelion (leontodon taraxacum) is one of the most difficult of the garden and field weeds to eradicate here; I have seen a hay-field literally white with it when in seed. Its root is sold at St. John's, in spring, by children who gather it in the gardens and fields, and in the absence of other fresh vegetables, after a long winter, it is much relished as a salad.

Sir Richard Henry Bonnycastle / Newfoundland in 1842

Fiddlehead

Fern Family

Matteuccia struthiopteris
Also called Ostrich-fern.
 Found in low-lying wooded areas, especially
along streams. Nova Scotia to British Columbia
and parts of the United States.
 The new, unfurled fronds appear in March or
April and are popularly known as 'fiddleheads';
they are a Maritime food specialty.
 Named *Matteuccia* in honour of an Italian
professor of physics.

THE MEN CAUGHT fish and hunted moose when they could. In the spring we made
maple sugar. We ate fiddle heads, grapes and even the leaves of trees to allay the pangs of
hunger. On one occasion some poisonous weeds were eaten along with the fiddle heads;
one or two died, and Dr. Earle had all he could do to save my life.
 Peter Fisher / Sketches of New Brunswick 1825

Fir

Pine Family / Pinaceae

BALSAM FIR / *Abies balsamea*
Also called White Fir; Silver Pine; Blister-pine.
Distinguishing features a medium-sized tree
(shrub-like in Arctic regions) with fragrant
leaves.

A prolific species, Alberta to eastern Canada
and the United States. A valuable commercial
species.
    Alpine Fir / *Abies lasiocarpa* is the only true
fir in the Rocky Mountains. Cascade Fir / *Abies
amabilis* is native to the west coast.

THEY [the Indians of Acadia] injure themselves very frequently, but Nature has placed
under the bark of the Balsam-fir, trees which are very common in all parts of Acadia, a
marvelous remedy for all their wounds; it is a Turpentine, finer in quality, & more
balsamic than that obtained from Venice, & it is found wherever it might be needed for a
dressing. If the Indians break their Arms or Legs, the bones are reset evenly, & large pads
of soft fine moss are made, which are saturated with their Turpentine, & wrapped around
the broken limb; outside of that is placed a piece of Birch-bark, which readily conforms to
the shape of the part; splints are not forgotten, &, to hold all this secure, they use long
strips of thinner bark which make suitable bandages. The Patient is then laid in position
on a bed of moss, & this method always succeeds very well.
    Sieur de Dièreville / Relation of the Voyage to Port Royal 1708

IT MUCH PLEASED ME to observe the manner in which the inhabitants [of Montreal]
kept Holy Thursday, which they term *La Fête Dieu*. On the evening preceding that day, I
could not conceive the reason that the people were bringing cart loads of small firs into
the city; but judge how great was my surprize in the morning, when I went to the parade,
to find the streets swept as clean as possible, these trees stuck in the ground on each side,
and so contrived that their tops united, that every street had the appearance of a grove,
and upon enquiry found it was intended for the celebration of this great festival.
    Thomas Anburey / Travels 1789

TRAVELLERS in the bush rise with the sun, and couch with the twilight. Our blankets
were spread at sun-down, under the tent, on a bed of sapin, the sweet-smelling fir of
Canada, whose tender branches are preferred for this purpose, and a very soft and
aromatic couch they make ...
    We retired to our pine-branch bed very early, and obtained a little rest; but the
mosquitoes and sand-flies were not disposed to sleep themselves, and seemed determined
that we should not.
    Sir Richard Henry Bonnycastle / The Canadas in 1841

Fireweed

Evening Primrose Family / Onagraceae

FIREWEED or GREAT WILLOW HERB /
Epilobium angustifolium (illustrated)
Found from Baffin Island, south, with sub-
species throughout Canada and south.
   In addition to the usual rose-purple form
there is a white-flowered form. Fireweed is the
floral emblem of the Yukon.
   Mrs Traill may be referring to Pilewort /
Erechtites hieracifolia, also called Fireweed.
COMMON EVENING PRIMROSE /
Oenothera biennis
Also called Night Willow Herb.
   It has forms with yellow to orange flowers.
Found throughout Canada, and south; usually
on dry open sites.

The biennial oenothera (*Oenothera biennis* L.) grows in abundance on open woody hills,
and fallow fields. An old Frenchman, who accompanied me as I was collecting its seeds,
could not sufficiently praise its property of healing wounds. The leaves of the plant must
be crushed and then laid on the wound.
   Peter Kalm / Travels into North America 1753–61

THE YOUNG LEAVES [of the Fireweed], under the name of L'Herbe Fret, are used, by
the Canadian voyagers, as a Pot-herb.
   John Richardson / Franklin: Narrative of a Journey 1823

THE FIRE-WEED, a species of tall thistle of rank and unpleasant scent, is the first plant
that appears when the ground has been freed from timbers by fire: if a piece of land lies
untilled the first summer after its being chopped, the following spring shows you a
smothering crop of this vile weed. The next plant you notice is the sumach, with its
downy stalks, and head of deep crimson velvety flowers, forming an upright obtuse
bunch at the extremity of the branches: the leaves turn scarlet towards the latter end of
the summer. This shrub, though really very ornamental, is regarded as a great pest in old
clearings, where the roots run and send up suckers in abundance. The raspberry and wild
gooseberry are next seen, and thousands of strawberry plants of different varieties carpet
the ground, and mingle with the grasses of the pastures. I have been obliged this spring to
root out with remorseless hand hundreds of sarsaparilla plants, and also the celebrated
ginseng, which grows abundantly in our woods: it used formerly to be an article of
export to China from the States, the root being held in high estimation by the Chinese.
   Catharine Parr Traill / The Backwoods of Canada 1836

Fungi

The Fungi are a group of simple plants which
have no green colouring; the mushrooms are
probably the best known.
MEADOW MUSHROOM / *Agaricus campestris*
This is a common mushroom and a member of
the Family Agaricaceae.

AS A MOST potent Poison they [the Acadians] regard
The Mushroom; not by eating it would they
Make widows of their wives. This item I
Will pass; reasons they may have had;
Too many People have made painful tests.
As for myself, I found them very good,
And, without ill effect, I ate my fill,
While with compassion all regarded me;
Salad's another thing they do not like,
And that was my advantage too.
   Sieur de Dièreville / Relation of the Voyage to Port Royal 1708

BESIDES GAINING a little money with my pen, I practised a method of painting birds
and butterflies upon the white, velvety surface of the large fungi, that grow plentifully
upon the bark of the sugar-maple. These had an attractive appearance, and my brother,
who was a captain in one of the provincial regiments, sold a great many of them among
the officers, without saying by whom they were painted. One rich lady in Peterborough,
long since dead, ordered two dozen to send as curiosities to England. These, at one
shilling each, enabled me to buy shoes for the children, who, during our bad times, had
been forced to dispense with these necessary coverings.
   Susanna Moodie / Roughing it in the Bush 1852

SUNDAY, August 31st [1862] ... Retire, after mushroom supper. Monday, September
1st ... In the night Messiter, having nightmare from mushrooms, jumped up under the
impression that Indians were in the tent, rushed out shouting and seizes Voudrie (in shirt
only).
   Walter Butler Cheadle / Journal 1862–3

Garlic, Onion, Leek

Lily Family / *Liliaceae*

These are all strong-smelling herbs growing from a bulb.

WILD GARLIC / *Allium canadense*
Also called Meadow Garlic.
Distinguishing features Grass-like leaves and a few pink or white flowers mixed with bulblets.

It and similar species such as Nodding Onion / *Allium cernuum* are found throughout much of Canada and the United States. May to July.

WILD LEEK / *Allium tricoccum* (illustrated)
Also called Ramps, Three-seeded Leek.
Distinguishing features Broad pungent leaves, greenish-white flower heads, and a strong-smelling bulb.

Found in rich woods, southern Manitoba to Nova Scotia (not Prince Edward Island), and south.

OF THE VEGETABLES this place produceth we benefited by none except the Spruce tree of which we made beer, and wild Garlick; the latter must have been in tolerable plenty by the quantity the Natives brought us toward the latter part of our stay. They do not make use of it themselves, but happening to see our people pull up some and eat, they brought some the next day to sell; this being bought incouraged other[s] to colle[c]t, so that it soon became a general article in trade and was the occasion of our having it in such plenty; for we neither knew where to go for it, nor had we time to collect it. This with some Nettles that grew about the Villages [of Nootka Sound] were the only Vegetable I saw fit for the pot, but there [were] others that are known to the Natives and make a part of their food especially firn roots, a root of a licorice taste and some others unknown to me which I saw them pull up and eat without so much as shaking of the dirt.
Captain James Cook / Journals 1776–80

APRIL 11 I discovered a quantity of wild leeks just shooting up out of the earth, of which I gathered a good many. I was unfortunate in this, my first essay on vegetable diet, for they heated me to such a degree, that I was for some time afraid they had possessed some deleterious quality; but the intolerably high flavour of the plant quieted my apprehensions. I was in a burning fever, at the same time quite sure that I had eaten nothing but leeks. Though they abounded all over the woods, for a long time afterwards I was too well satisfied with my first dose ever to try another.
Sir George Head / Forest Scenes and Incidents 1829

AT LAST we came to a lake filled near the upper end with a luxuriant growth of rushes and wild garlic, among which the water proved on trial to be nearly free from salt. This, it is said, is usually the case where such vegetation is found, – whether because the plants have a purifying quality, or because they mark the position of wholesome springs, I did not happen to ascertain.
Earl of Southesk / Saskatchewan and the Rocky Mountains 1859–60

Ginseng

Ginseng Family / Araliaceae

Panax quinquefolius
Also called Red-berry.
Distinguishing features three compound leaves each with 5-toothed leaflets: pale greenish flower clusters; thick fleshy forked root.

Found in rich woods, Quebec, Ontario, Minnesota, and south. July to August. The wild plant is now rare due to over-harvesting, however Ginseng is being grown extensively for commercial purposes.

The name 'Ginseng' is from the Chinese and probably means 'image of man,' alluding to the shape of the root.

THESE INDIANS [around Fort St Joseph, in what is now Michigan], who have from the earliest times applied themselves more than others to the study of medicine, make great account of the root ginseng, and are persuaded that this plant has the virtue of rendering women fruitful. I do not believe however that it is for this reason they have given it the name of *Abesoatchenza* which signifies a child; it owes this name at least among the Iroquois to the figure of its root. Your Grace has no doubt seen what Father [Lafitau] who first brought it into France, has written of it under the name *Aureliana Canadensis*: it is at least in shape exactly the same with that which comes from China, and which the Chinese bring from Corea and Tartary. The name they give it, and which signifies *the likeness of man*; the virtues attributed to it, and which have been experienced in Canada by such as have used it, and the conformity of the climate are a strong presumption that did we only believe it to come from China, it would be as much esteemed as that which the Chinese sell us. And perhaps too it owes its little credit amongst us, to its growing in a country which belongs to us, and that it wants the advantage of being in every respect a foreign commodity.

Pierre-François-Xavier de Charlevoix / Journal of a Voyage 1744

ONE ARTICLE of commerce the Canadians had, by their own imprudence, rendered altogether unprofitable. Ginseng was first discovered in the woods of Canada in 1718. It was from that country exported to Canton, where its quality was pronounced to be equal to that of the ginseng procured in Corea or in Tartary, and a pound of this plant, which before sold in Quebec for twentypence, became, when its value was once ascertained, worth one pound and tenpence sterling. The export of this article alone is said to have amounted, in 1752, to twenty thousand pounds sterling. But the Canadians, eager suddenly to enrich themselves, reaped this plant in May, when it should not have been gathered until September, and dried it in ovens, when its moisture should have been gradually evaporated in the shade. This fatal mistake arising from cupidity, and in some measure from ignorance, ruined the sale of their ginseng, among the only people upon earth who are partial to its use, and at an early period cut off from the colony a new branch of trade, which, under proper regulations, might have been essentially productive.

George Heriot / Travels through the Canadas 1807

Grape

Wild Grape / Vitaceae

The genus *Vitis* is represented in Canada and parts of the United States by *Vitis aestivalis, Vitis labrusca, Vitis riparia* and *Vitis vulpina* (illustrated).

SUMMER GRAPE / *Vitis aestivalis* is found in southern and eastern Ontario.

RIVERBANK or FROST GRAPE / *Vitis riparia* grows from Nova Scotia to Manitoba, and south. The other two species are thought to be introductions from the United States.

All the grape vines climb with tendrils; they differ in the form of the leaves and skin of the grapes.

[THE SAVAGES brought] … grapes newly gathered, because they had seen Frenchmen eat of them at Chouakoet. Which the other savages seeing that knew it not, they brought more of them than one would, emulating one another; and for recompense of this their kindness, there was set on their foreheads a fillet, or band, of paper, wet with spittle, of which they were very proud. It was shewed them, in pressing the grape into a glass, that of that we did make the wine which we did drink. We would have made them to eat of the grape, but, having taken it into their mouths, they spitted it out, so ignorant is this people of the best thing that God hath given to man next to bread.

THE SAVAGES of the other side did bring fish, and grapes within baskets made of rushes, for to exchange with some of our wares. The said Monsieur de Poutrincourt, seeing the grapes there marvellously fair, commanded him that waited on his chamber to lay up in the barque a burthen of the vines from whence the said grapes were taken. Our apothecary, M. Louis Hébert, desirous to inhabit in those countries, had pulled out a good quantity of them, to the end to plant them in Port Royal, where none of them are, although the soil be there very fit for vines. Which nevertheless (by a dull forgetfulness) was not done, to the great discontent of the said Monsieur de Poutrincourt and of us all.
  Marc Lescarbot / History of New France 1609 (both passages)

I WILL TELL YOU, by the way, that the vine grows here [near Port Dover, Patterson's Creek] only in sand, on the banks of lakes and rivers, but although it has no cultivation it does not fail to produce grapes in great quantities as large and as sweet as the finest of France. We even made wine of them, with which M. Dollier said holy mass all winter, and it was as good as vin de Grave. It is a heavy, dark wine like the latter. Only red grapes are seen here, but in so great quantities, that we found places where one could easily have made 25 or 30 hogsheads of wine.
  François Dollier de Casson and René de Bréhant de Galinée / Journal 1669–70

THE WILD GRAPEVINES (*Vitis labrusca & vulpina*) grow quite plentifully in the woods. In all other parts of Canada they plant them in the gardens, near arbors and summer houses. The latter are made entirely of laths, over which the vines climb with their tendrils, and cover them entirely with their foliage so as to shelter them entirely from the heat of the sun. They are very refreshing and cool in summer.
  Peter Kalm / Travels into North America 1753–61

Greens

SCURVY GRASS

The name has been used for both *Cochlearia officinalis* and *Barbarea verna* (illustrated). In Baffin's *Voyages* the former is obviously referred to, as it grows along the Arctic coast, on sands or salt marshes. *Barbarea verna*, also called Bitter-cress, is a weed, usually found in fields. Both belong to the Mustard Family.

VETCH

Vicia americana is one of the dozen vetches now found in Canada – British Columbia to Quebec, including James Bay – and the United States. All the vetches have leaves ending in tendrils, and small, pea-like flowers and belong to the Leguminosae.

PURSLANE

Portulaca oleracea is a low spreading plant with small fleshy leaves and yellow flowers which do not always open. It was a common pot-herb in Europe and is generally thought to have been introduced in North America. Now widely distributed. It belongs to the Portulacaceae.

SORREL

The name Sorrel is used for the genera Oxalis and Rumex. *Rumex acetosella* (Sheep Sorrel) also belongs to the Mustard Family. It is often used in salads. Mrs Traill's wood-cress may be the common *Deutaria diphylla*, toothwort, also called pepper-root, crinkleroot.

THE NEXT DAY, going on shoare on a little iland [in the vicinity of Cocking Sound], we found great abundance of the herbe called scurvie grasse, which we boyled in beere, and so dranke thereof, vsing it also in sallets, with sorrell and orpen [stone crop] which here groweth in abundance; by meanes hereof, and the blessing of God, all our men within eight or nine dayes space were in perfect health, and so continued till our arriuall in England.

William Baffin / Voyages 1612–22

AND NOW I must remind you of God's goodness towards us in sending us those green vetches that I mentioned earlier. For even the sickest man, those who for the last two or three months could not have bestirred themselves even if their lives depended on it, were now up and around. The other men were also getting stronger, and it was wonderful to see how rapidly they recovered. Twice a day, we went to gather the herb or leaf of the vetches as they first appeared out of the ground. After they were washed and boiled, we ate them with oil and vinegar that had been frozen. It was an excellent and refreshing sustenance, and most of us ate nothing else. Sometimes we would crush them and mix the juice with our beverage; sometimes we ate them raw with our bread.

Captain Thomas James / Strange and Dangerous Voyage 1631–2

THERE WAS NEVER Anchorite more abstemious than this poor captive on that journey [Père Jogues after his capture by the Iroquois, just prior to his martyrdom]; his living was only a little wild purslane which he went to gather in the fields, with which he made a soup without other seasoning than clear water. They gave him, indeed, certain seeds to eat, – but so insipid and so dangerous that they served as a very quick poison to those who knew not how to prepare them; and he would not touch them.

Jérôme Lalemant / Jesuit Relations 1647

THE WOOD-CRESS, or as it is called by some, ginger-cress, is a pretty white cruciform flower; it is highly aromatic in flavour; the root is white and fleshy, having the pungency of horse-radish. The leaves are of a sad green …

Catharine Parr Traill / The Backwoods of Canada 1836

Groundnut

Pea Family / Leguminosae

GROUNDNUT / *Apios americana*
Also called Wild Bean; Micmac Potato; Sequb-bun; Bog Potato; Ground-, Trailing-, or Potato-pea; Pig-, Dacotah-, or Indian-potato; White Apple; Traveler's-delight.
Distinguishing features a beautiful climbing vine or straggling plant with fragrant maroon or brownish flowers, leaves compounded of 5 to 7 pointed leaflets. Rhizomes have up to a dozen highly edible sweet tubers of up to 3 inches in diameter.
Found in damp ground, Nova Scotia to western Ontario, Minnesota, Texas etc. July to September.

IN THE MIDDLE of March ... our friends launched their boat, which endured the violence of the rivers and even of the sea; nor did they fear ... to ascend the river flowing into French Bay, to gather acorns and the Chiquebi root in the forest. The *Chiquebi* root is peculiar to this coast, and is not unlike our potatoes, but more pleasant and useful for eating; its numerous bulbs, joined by a slender thread, grow deep in the earth. However, our collectors found that all the spots where this root grew had been already visited by the Savages.
Pierre Biard / Jesuit Relations 1612–14

THESE ROOTS ... grow readily near oak trees. They are like truffles, but better, and grow under the ground strung to each other like a rosary.
Pierre Biard / Jesuit Relations 1611–16

PADDLING DOWN a picturesque Nova-Scotian stream called the Shubenacadie some ten years since in an Indian canoe, it occurred to me to ask the steersman the proper Micmac pronunciation of the name. He replied, 'We call 'em "Segeebenacadie." Plenty wild potatoes – segeeben – once grew here.' 'Well, "acadie," Paul, what does that mean?' I inquired. 'Means – where you find 'em,' said the Indian.

ON THIS BROOK I first saw the blossoms and tendrils of a beautiful climbing plant which grew up luxuriantly amongst the bushes, and encircled small stems to a consider-able height – the Indian potato-plant (*Apios tuberosa*) – one of the sources of food used by the old Indians before they left the woods and their forest fare for the neighbourhood of civilization, and adopted its food, clothing, and depraving associations. The flowers are like those of the sweet pea, and arranged in a whorl, possessing a pleasant though rather faint smell. The cluster of bulbs at its root, called potatoes, are of about the average size of small new potatoes, and have a flavour like a chestnut.
Campbell Hardy / Forest Life in Acadie 1869 *(both passages)*

Harebell, Common Bluebell

Bluebell or Harebell Family / Campanulaceae

HAREBELL / *Campanula rotundifolia*
Also called Blue Bells of Scotland; Thimbles;
Lady's-thimble; Heath- or Witches'-bells;
Round-leaved Bellflower.
Distinguishing feature the flowering stems are
very slender (hairlike) and wiry.
   Found in rocky or sandy locations, Alaska,
Yukon, Alberta to Newfoundland. June to
September.

Several other common Harebells are Arctic
Harebell / *Campanula uniflora*, Alpine
Bellflower / *Campanula lasiocarpa*, Creeping
Harebell / *Campanula rapunculoides*, and
Scouler's Harebell / *Campanula scouleri*
(British Columbia and south).
   'Harebell' is supposedly a mis-spelling of
'Hairbell'; referring to the hair-thin stems.
'Campanula' from Latin, meaning little bell.
   The purple weeds referred to by Southesk are
probably wild bergamot.

PUSHING OUR WAY through the bushes, we came to a small opening in the underwood,
so thickly grown over with wild Canadian roses in full blossom, that the air was
impregnated with a delightful odour. In the centre of this bed of sweets rose the humble
mound that protected the bones of the red man from the ravenous jaws of the wolf and
the wild cat. It was completely covered with stones, and from among the crevices had
sprung a tuft of blue harebells, waving as wild and free as if they grew among the bonny
red heather on the glorious hills of the North or shook their tiny bells to the breeze on the
broom-encircled commons of England.
   The harebell had always from a child been with me a favourite flower; and the first
sight of it in Canada, growing upon that lonely grave, so flooded my soul with remem-
brances of the past, that in spite of myself the tears poured freely from my eyes.
   Susanna Moodie / Roughing it in the Bush 1852

OF ALL MY HORSES he [le pauvre Bichon] is the only one that eats flowers, and I have
had many a laugh at seeing the old fellow wander off the track to browse on a tuft of
blue-bells or tiger-lilies. He particularly delights in certain purple weeds that grow in
such large tufts as to be often mistaken at a distance for buffaloes. Why is it absurd that a
horse should eat flowers? I know not why, but it is. An ancient philosopher died of
laughter at the sight of an ass eating roses.
   The Earl of Southesk / Saskatchewan and the Rocky Mountains 1859–60

Hawthorn

Rose Family / Rosaceae

At least 300 species of Hawthorn are found in
Canada and the United States and it is often
difficult to separate the different species. The
centre of distribution is in the eastern United
States.
ROUND-LEAVED HAWTHORN / *Crataegus
rotundifolia*
One of the widest-ranging hawthorns.
Distinguishing features rounded wide-
spreading shrub or tree with numerous thorns,
white flowers, and red fruit.
   Found along roadsides and in open woods,
Maritimes to British Columbia, and south.
Flowers in May.

CLOSE TO the Upper end of the Town [Queenston] the spot was pointed out to me where
the Brave General Brock was killed – It is quite near to the road and is marked by a
number of thorn bushes, which form a kind of circle – They were not however planted on
that account, but have grown here long before that circumstance taking place.
   John Goldie / Diary of a Journey through Upper Canada 1819

THE THORN or hawthorn is also found [in the vicinity of St John's], and hedges of the
English whitethorn or May have been introduced, and would thrive extremely well if it
were not for the great difficulty attendant upon their protection from cattle and goats. In
winter these fences are exposed also to plunder, as no wood grows near the city, and the
really heavy cost of fencing appears so lightly valued, that no law has hitherto been made
to protect them, though every boy who takes his dogs to the woods to draw home fuel on
a sledge or catamaran, as it is called, very unceremoniously wrenches a stick or so out of
the first fence in his way, and will even deliberately cut down a whole pannel or length, if
there is a better road to be had through a field than the common highway.
   Sir Richard Henry Bonnycastle / Newfoundland in 1842

Hemlock

Pine Family, Conifers / Pinaceae

There are four species of hemlock in North America; three are found in Canada. They can be distinguished from other native coniferous trees because their needle-like leaves are attached to the twig by tiny thread-like stems.

WESTERN HEMLOCK / *Tsuga heterophylla*
Also called British Columbia Hemlock; Alaska Pine.

A large graceful tree occurring throughout the coastal and interior wet areas in British Columbia and southward. Valuable for pulpwood.

MOUNTAIN HEMLOCK / *Tsuga mertensiana*
Also called Black Hemlock.

A small tree found throughout the western coastal belt and in some mountain areas.

EASTERN HEMLOCK / *Tsuga canadensis* (illustrated)
Also called Hemlock; Canadian Hemlock; Hemlock Spruce; White Hemlock.

A medium-sized tree ranging from Nova Scotia to western Ontario and south.

WHEN WE HAD SATISFIED ourselves with the fish, one of the people approached, with a kind of ladle in one hand, containing oil, and in the other something that resembled the inner rind of the cocoa-nut, but of a lighter colour; this he dipped in the oil, and, having eaten it, indicated by his gestures how palatable he thought it. He then presented me with a small piece of it, which I chose to taste in its dry state, though the oil was free from any unpleasant smell. A square cake of this was next produced, when a man took it to the water near the house, and having thoroughly soaked it, he returned, and, after he had pulled it to pieces like oakum, put it into a well-made trough, about three feet long, nine inches wide, and five deep: he then plentifully sprinkled it with salmon oil ... The chief partook of it with great avidity ... This dish is considered by these people as a great delicacy; and on examination, I discovered it to consist of the inner rind of the hemlock tree, taken off early in summer, and put into a frame, which shapes it into cakes of fifteen inches long, ten broad, and half an inch thick; and in this form I should suppose it may be preserved for a great length of time. This discovery satisfied me respecting the many hemlock trees which I had observed stripped of their bark.

Alexander Mackenzie / Voyages from Montreal 1801

I HAVE CAMPED OUT, I dare say, hundreds of times, both in winter and summer; and I never caught cold yet. I recommend, from experience, a hemlock-bed, and hemlock-tea, with a dash of whiskey in it, merely to assist the flavour, as the best preventive.

Samuel Strickland / Twenty-Seven Years in Canada West 1853

HEMLOCK BARK, possessing highly astringent properties, is much used in America for tanning purposes, almost entirely superseding that of the oak. Its surface is very rough with deep grooves between the scales. Of a light pearly gray outside, it shows a madder brown tint when chipped. The sojourner in the woods seeks the dry and easily detached bark which clings to an old dead hemlock as a great auxiliary to his stock of fuel for the campfire; it burns readily and long, emitting an intense heat, and so fond are the old Indians of sitting round a small conical pile of the ignited bark in their wigwams, that it bears in their language the sobriquet of 'the old Grannie.'

Campbell Hardy / Forest Life in Acadie 1869

Hepatica

Crowfoot Family / Ranunculaceae

ROUND-LOBED HEPATICA / *Hepatica americana*

Also called Kidney Liver-leaf; Noble Liverwort; Heart Liverwort; Three-leaf Liverwort; Livermoss; Mouse-ears; Crystalwort; Golden Trefoil; Ivy-flower; Herb Trinity; Squirrel-cup.

Distinguishing features white, pink or mauve flowers; three-lobed leaves. The leaves were thought to resemble the liver by ancient writers, hence the name 'hepatica' from the Latin 'hepar,' liver. The supposed likeness of the leaves to the heart or kidneys accounts for other popular names.

Found growing in tufts in woodlands, such as sugar bush. Nova Scotia to Manitoba, and south. Flowers March to May.

The only other North American species is *Hepatica acutiloba*, the Sharp-lobed Hepatica or Heart Liver-leaf, Liverwort, Spring-beauty, May-flower. Both species occurred in Mrs Traill's district.

THE HEPATICA is the first flower of the Canadian spring: it gladdens us with its tints of azure, pink, and white, early in April, soon after the snows have melted from the earth. The Canadians call it snow-flower, from its coming so soon after the snow disappears. We see its gay tufts of flowers in the open clearings and the deep recesses of the forests; its leaves are also an enduring ornament through the open months of the year; you see them on every grassy mound and mossy root; the shades of blue are very various and delicate, the white anthers forming a lovely contrast with the blue petals.

Catharine Parr Traill / The Backwoods of Canada 1836

Jack-in-the-Pulpit

Arum Family / Araceae

Arisaema species
Several similar species or subspecies are called
Jack-in-the-Pulpit or Indian Turnip. They all
have a flap or 'spathe' overhanging a central
green spike of flowers (spadix) – hence, *Jack* in
his *pulpit*. The root is strongly acrid.

Found in moist woods, Nova Scotia, Prince
Edward Island to Ontario, Manitoba, and
south. Flowers April to June. The fruit is a head
of scarlet berries which ripen June to July.

The illustration is of *Arisaema triphyllum*.

AGAIN on another occasion we had a fright, which afterwards turned into a laughing
matter. Some little children of the savages had got some roots called *Ooxrat*, like a small
carrot or peeled chestnut, which they had just pulled up to take to their lodges. A young
French boy, living with us, had asked them for some and had eaten one or two. At first he
thought the taste quite pleasant, but shortly afterwards he felt great pain in his mouth,
like a burning, prickling flame, and a great deal of watery humour and phlegm continually dropped from his mouth so that he thought he was about to die. And in truth we did
not know what to do about it, being ignorant of the cause of this symptom, and fearing
lest he had eaten some poisonous root. But when we spoke to the savages about it and
asked for their advice they had the rest of the roots brought to see what they were, and
when they had seen and recognized them, they began to laugh, saying that there was no
danger nor any evil result to be feared, but rather good, if it were not for those stinging
and burning pains in the mouth. They use these roots to purge the phlegm and moisture
in the head of old people and to clear the complexion; but in order to avoid the stinging
pain they first cook it in hot ashes and then eat it without feeling any pain afterwards, and
it does them all the good in the world. I am sorry that I did not bring some of it here to
France on account of the use which I think would have been made of it.

Gabriel Sagard / The Long Journey to the Country of the Hurons 1632

Labrador Tea

Heath Family / Ericaceae

Ledum groenlandicum
Also called Wisha-capucca.
Distinguishing features an erect shrub with
leathery oblong leaves which have rolled edges;
their underside is covered with a rusty 'wool';
white flower clusters.

Found in bogs or wet thickets, Greenland,
Labrador to Yukon, British Columbia, northern United States. May to August.

Similar species are *Ledum palustre* and
Ledum glandulosum

'Ledol, a toxic compound that can induce
cramps and paralysis, has been isolated from
the leaves of all of the Ledum species. Possibly
in the low concentrations of the pioneers' brew,
this substance may have produced restorative
effects similar to those resulting from caffeine
in tea.' *Wild Flowers of British Columbia*,
P 373.

THE PLANT, by the *Indians* called Wizzekapukka, is used by them, and the *English* as a
Medicine, in nervous and scorbutick Disorders; its most apparent and immediate Effect,
is promoting Digestion, and causing a keen Appetite. To this Plant, the Surgeons
residing at the Factories, ascribe all the Qualities of Rhubarb; it is a strong Aromatick,
and tastes pleasantly enough when drank as a Tea, which is the common Way of using it.

Henry Ellis / A Voyage to Hudson's-Bay 1748

[NEAR STARVATION in the Lake Athabasca area David Thompson and his companion
are forced to eat the inside fat from slain eagles, which makes them sick.] In the night we
were both awakened by a violent dysentry ... I filled the pewter basin with Labrador tea,
and by means of hot stones made a strong infusion, [and] drank it as hot as I could, which
very much relieved me.

David Thompson / Travels in Western North America 1784–1812

OUR ONLY LUXURY [while navigating the Polar Sea in two canoes] now was a little salt,
which had long been our substitute both for bread and vegetables. Since our departure
from Point Lake we had boiled the Indian tea plant, *ledum palustre*, which produced a
beverage in smell much resembling rhubarb; notwithstanding which we found it refreshing, and were gratified to see this plant flourishing abundantly, though of dwarfish
growth, on the sea-shore.

Sir John Franklin / Narrative of a Journey 1823

Lady's Slipper

Orchis Family / Orchidaceae

YELLOW LADY'S SLIPPER / *Cypripedium calceolus*
Also called Downey Ladies'-slipper; Yellow Moccasin-flower; Whip-poor-will's Shoe; Yellows; Slipper-root; Indian Shoe; Noah's-ark; Ducks; American Valerian.

'Cypripedium' from the Greek: 'Cyprus,' the reputed birthplace of Venus, and 'pedilon,' sock or slipper.
Distinguishing features the 'pouch' is always golden-yellow despite local variations in the size of flowers and colour of lateral petals.

Found, often growing in colonies, in rich woods or bogs; the aggregate species from the Yukon to Newfoundland and south.

RAM'S-HEAD LADY'S SLIPPER / *Cypripedium arietinum* has a small conical pouch, somewhat distorted at the upper end, giving the appearance of a ram's head. Found in bogs and damp woods, Saskatchewan to Quebec, Nova Scotia, and south.

Pierre de Charlevoix referred to the Lady's-slipper in 1744 as 'Le Sabot de la Vierge.'

THE MOCCASIN FLOWER or lady's slipper ... is one of our most remarkable flowers, both on account of its beauty and its singularity of structure. Our plains and dry sunny pastures produce several varieties; among these, the *Cypripedium pubescens*, or yellow moccasin, and the *C. Arietinum* are the most beautiful of the species ... The upper petals [of the former] consist of two short and two long ... the short ones stand erect, like a pair of ears; the long or lateral pair are three times the length of the former, very narrow, and elegantly twisted, like the spiral horns of the Walachian ram: on raising a thick yellow fleshy sort of lid in the middle of the flower, you perceive the exact face of an Indian hound, perfect in all its parts – the eyes, nose, and mouth; below this depends an open sack, slightly gathered round at the opening, which gives it a hollow and prominent appearance; the inside of this bag is delicately dashed with deep crimson spots ... the elegant colour and silken texture of the lower lip or bag renders this flower very much more beautiful to my taste than the purple and white variety, though the latter is much more striking on account of the size of the flower and leaves ...

The formation of this species resembles the other, only with this difference, the horns are not twisted, and the face is that of a monkey; even the comical expression of the animal is preserved with such admirable fidelity as to draw a smile from everyone that sees the odd restless-looking visage, with its prominent round black eyes peering forth from under its covering.

These plants ... are described with some little variations by Pursh, who, however, likens the face of the latter to that of a sheep: if a sheep sat for the picture methinks it must have been the most mischievous of the flock.

Catharine Parr Traill / The Backwoods of Canada 1836

THE *Lady's slipper*, both of the purplish and the more ordinary kind, is found in the woods in Canada, but it is not a very common plant. The English name must originally, I apprehend, have been *Our Lady's slipper*, (as, by a not very dissimilar process of formation, we have the term *Lady Day*,) for the French call the flower *le sabot de la Sainte Vierge*; and the translation is by no means happy; for the blossom, which has but a disputable resemblance to a slipper, and especially to that of a lady, very closely resembles in form the *wooden sabot* worn often by the peasantry in muddy roads, and derived from their progenitors in France.

Bishop George Mountain / Songs of the Wilderness 1846

Lily

Lily Family / Liliaceae

RED LILY / *Lilium philadelphicum*
The Earl of Southesk describes a variation of the
Red Lily, the Western Red Lily / *Lilium
philadelphicum* var. *andinum* (illustrated). Its
flowers are orange, upward-facing, with leaves
scattered along the stem.

Found in dry locations, British Columbia to
western Quebec, and south. June to July.

Lilium tigrinum is also called Tiger-lily; it
occurs as a garden escape in eastern Canada and
the United States.

All our native species have edible bulbs.

ON THE 5TH of the same month of November, a tall young Savage, returning from
beaver hunting, called upon us, crying out that he was dying of hunger. He brought a
number of roots, among them several bulbs of the red lily variety, of which there are a
great many here. We gave him something, and tasted these bulbs, which are very good to
eat; he made no other sauce than to boil them in a little water without salt, which the
Savages do not use.

Paul Le Jeune / Jesuit Relations 1632–3

This was a prairie country [near Qu'Appelle] of sand and crisp grass ... Flowers of the
gayest colour enlivened the landscape. The most common were the small tiger-lilies and
the roses, and next came blue-bells and white strawberry blossoms. Sometimes acres and
acres were covered with intermingled masses of the orange lily and the pendulous
blue-bell, the whole of them so short of stem that the glory of the flowers combined with
the rich greenness of their leaves, and it seemed as if a vast oriental carpet had been
thrown upon the plain.

The Earl of Southesk / Saskatchewan and the Rocky Mountains 1859–60

Lupine, Lupin

Pea Family / Leguminosae

Most North American lupines are western. Twenty-three species occur in British Columbia, of which the commonest is probably the Silky Lupine / *Lupinus sericeus*. The name comes from the Latin 'sericus,' meaning silk, and referring to the dense covering of hairs on the leaves and stems.

Found, often in poor soil, west coast to southwestern Alberta, and south.

WILD LUPINE / *Lupinus perennis* (illustrated) grows in some areas of Ontario. Its seeds are sometimes cooked like domestic peas; they can, however, be poisonous due to the presence of the alkaloid *lupinine*.

Other lupines growing wild in eastern Canada and the Maritimes are considered to be garden escapes.

THE FOLLOWING DAY we made a short portage over the bite or neck of Cape Disappointment to a small lake, out of which flowed a narrow stream to the bay northward of the cape, which we descended, and put on shore at dusk on Cape Foulweather. The rain fell in torrents without intermission throughout the day. We sent the canoe to the Columbia from this place in the evening, the Indians being anxious to return hastily as we had not the means of feeding them. The wind about midnight increased to a hurricane with sleet and hail, and twice were we obliged to shift our camp, the sea rising so unusually high. We had no protection save what a few pine branches and our wet blankets afforded, and no food. Long ere daylight we were ready to leave Cape Foulweather, which name it truly deserves, and we walked along the sandy beach, sixteen miles to Whitbey Harbour, where we found the village deserted, our prospect not in the least bettered. We remained here several days, faring scantily on roots of *Sagittaria sagittifolia* [Long-beaked arrow-head] and *Lupinus littoralis*, called in the Chenook tongue *Somúchtan*, and from continual exposure to the cold and rain and the want of proper sustenance I became greatly reduced.

David Douglas / Journal 1823–7

Maidenhair Fern

Fern Family

Adiantum pedatum
Also called Capillaire; Lock-hair Fern.
Distinguishing features slender, creeping
rootstock; fan-shaped leaflets.

Found in woods, Alaska, British Columbia to
southwestern Alberta. Also Ontario to Newfoundland, except Prince Edward Island, and
south.

The Canada Maidenhair was 'cultivated with
great Care in the King's Garden at Paris' and
prescribed for consumption and coughs. Alice
M. Coats *The Treasury of Flowers,* quoting
from *A Compleat History of Druggs* by P.
Pomet, 1712.

MAIDENHAIR is as common in the Forrests of *Canada*, as Fern is in those of *France*, and
is esteem'd beyond that of other Countries; insomuch, that the Inhabitants of *Quebec*
prepare great quantities of its Syrup, which they send to *Paris, Nants, Rouan,* and
several other Cities in France.
Baron de Lahontan / New Voyages to North-America 1703

[THE HURONS at the Lorette Mission three leagues from Quebec] gather, toward the
end of August, quantities of a plant useful in pharmacy and of no mean value in Europe,
which druggists call 'Capillaire.'
Louis d'Avaugour / Jesuit Relations 1702–12

Maple

Maple Family / Aceraceae

SUGAR MAPLE / *Acer saccharum*
Also called Hard Maple; Rock Maple; Black, Curly- or Bird's-eye Maple; Sugar-tree. *Distinguishing features* familiar tall expansive tree; brilliant autumn foliage.

Found in rich soil, Ontario, Quebec, New Brunswick, and south. (Planted elsewhere.)

An extremely valuable hardwood, used for furniture, veneer, plywood, etc. The bird's-eye and curly maple used by cabinet makers are varieties. A good shade tree. Ornamental. The sap is the main source of maple syrup.

Species of maple are found in every Canadian province and in most American states. The sap of all the maples contains a form of sugar and in pioneer days all species were tapped.

A THING which has seemed to me very remarkable in the maple water is this, that if, by virtue of boiling, it is reduced to a third, it becomes a real syrup, which hardens to something like sugar, and takes on a reddish colour. It is formed into little loaves which are sent to France as a curiosity, and which in actual use serve very often as a substitute for French sugar. I have several times mixed it with brandy, cloves and cinnamon, and this makes a kind of very agreeable rossolis. The observation is worthy of note that there must be snow at the foot of the tree in order that it shall let its sweet water run; and it refuses to yield this liquid when the snow appears no more upon the ground.
Chrestien Le Clercq / New Relation of Gaspesia 1691

'TIS BUT FEW of the Inhabitants that have the patience to make Mapple-Water, for as common and usual things are always slighted, so there's scarce any body but Children that give themselves the trouble of gathering these Trees. To conclude, the North-Country *Mapples* have more Sap than those of the South Countries; but at the same time the Sap is not so sweet.
Baron de Lahontan / New Voyages to North-America 1703

STRAWBERRIES are no less plentiful in the fields everywhere [in Acadia], & one has the pleasure of eating them with a Sugar produced in the Country.
Instead of Canes, whose Pores secrete
White Sugar, brought here from afar,
Nature, for the Acadian, with kind
Forethought, has put some in the Sycamore [Maple].
When Springtime comes, this tree gives forth
A sweetish liquor from its bark,
And this, in each vicinity,
The Settlers all collect with care.
This seemed a pleasant brew to me
In copious draughts I drank it down;
And Lemons only did we need
To make it into Lemonade.
Sieur de Dièreville / Relation of the Voyage to Port Royal 1708

HEARING THAT sugar was made from Trees in Canada, and being thorough Loyalists, and not wishing to be mixed up with the Contest about to be carried on, we packed up our effects and came over to Canada …
Catharine White / Loyalist Narratives from Upper Canada c 1775

May Apple

Barberry Family / Berberidaceae

Podophyllum peltatum
Also called Wild Mandrake; Wild Lemon;
Indian- or Hog-apple; Devil's-apples;
Puck's-foot; Raccoon-berry.
Distinguishing features a tall stock branching
into 2 large spreading leaves; from the forked
joint hangs a single large waxy white flower.
The fruit is about 2 inches long, egg-shaped,
yellow.
   The fruit is edible but the root, leaves, and
stem are poisonous. Some writers praise the
flavour of May Apple; others say it is acid,
sickly, and evil-smelling.
   Found in woodland, Nova Scotia, western
Quebec, and southern Ontario west to Minnesota, and south. April to June.

THIS COUNTRY [around Georgian Bay] is very beautiful ... It is much intersected by
brooks, which flow into the lake; and there are a great many vines and plums, which are
very good; raspberries, strawberries, little wild apples, nuts and a kind of fruit which has
the form and color of small lemons, about the size of an egg. The plant that bears it is two
and a half feet tall and has three or four leaves, at the most, of the form of the fig-leaf, and
each plant bears only two apples ...
   Samuel de Champlain / Voyages and Explorations 1604–16

NIAGARA, 1792: Wed. 19th: I send you May apple seeds. I think it is the prettiest plant I
have seen; the leaves extremely large, of a bright green; the flower consists of five white
petals of the texture of orange flowers, but three times larger; ten yellow chives round a
large seed vessel, which becomes a fruit of the colour and near the size of a magnum
bonum plum, the seeds resembling a melon. The flower is on a short foot stalk, one or
two sitting between the leaves. They grow near the roots of old trees in good land. The
fruit is ripe in August.
   Monday, 31st August, 1795: The May apples are now a great luxury; I have had some
preserved, and the hurtleberries are ripe. Baron La Hontan says the root of the May
apples (or, as the French call them *citrons sauvages*) is poisonous.
   Elizabeth Simcoe / Diary 1792–6

Mayflower

Heath Family / Ericaceae

Epigaea repens
Also called Trailing Arbutus; Ground Laurel;
Mountain Pink; Gravel-plant; Crocus;
Shadflower.
Distinguishing features oval leathery ever-
green leaves, spreading over the ground. Flow-
ers pink or white.

Found in shady woods and on sheltered hill-
sides, Labrador, Newfoundland to southern
Manitoba, and south. Flowers March to May.

A number of other early-blooming plants are
popularly called Mayflower or May-flower, as
Anemone quinquefolia (Snowdrop, Wood-
anemone), *Claytonia virginica* (Spring
Beauty), and *Cardamine pratensis* (Meadow
Bittercress).

Mayflower is the floral emblem of Nova
Scotia.

THE GREEN GLOSSY LEAVES of the winter green, whose bright scarlet berries look like
clusters of coral on the snow, now [in spring] seem even brighter than they were – the
blue violet rises among the sheltered moss by the old tree roots, and the broad-leaved
adder tongue gives out its orange and purple blossoms to gladden the brown earth … The
May flowers of New Brunswick seldom blossom till June, which is rather an Irish thing of
them to do.

Emily Beavan / Life in the backwoods of New Brunswick 1845

WHAT HEART does not feel forgotten memories recalled, when, wandering along sunny
banks in the fir-woods, the first blossom of the fragrant May-flower is seen and culled?
'We bloom amid the snow,' is the motto of our province; and the May-flower (Epigaea
repens) is to us what the violet, sought in hedge-rows, is to our friends at home –
entailing the same close search for its retiring blossoms, and evoking the same feelings of
gladness and hope. And we cling to these balmy spring days all the more closely as we
dread the chill easterly wind, and the dark sea-fog which may cover us with its gloom on
the morrow.

Campbell Hardy / Forest Life in Acadie 1869

Milkweed

Milkweed Family / Asclepiadaceae

COMMON MILKWEED / *Asclepias syriaca*
Also called Petits cochons; Silkweed; Silky
Swallow-wort; Virginia Silk; Wild Cotton;
Butterfly-weed.
Distinguishing features hairy leaves and stout
stem yielding a bitter milky fluid; lilac-
coloured flowers which change to large
rough-coated seed-pods.
Found in dry soil along roadsides etc, Prince
Edward Island to southern Manitoba, and
south. June to August.

Showy Milkweed / *Asclepias speciosa* is
similar. It ranges from southern Manitoba to
British Columbia and south.
Young leaves, stems, and pods of the milkweed are edible. A good brown sugar is supposedly made from the flowers. The Monarch
Butterfly has a special relationship with the
milkweed. After its eggs are laid on the leaves,
the larvae feed on them and accumulate bitter
and toxic glucosides which later make the
Monarch Butterfly distasteful to birds.

[BOTH THE PEOPLE of Canada and Hochelaga have] yet at this time excellent hemp,
which the ground produceth of itself. It is higher, finer, whiter, and stronger than ours in
these our parts. But that of the Armouchiquois beareth at the top of the stalk thereof a
pod, filled with a kind of cotton, like unto silk, in which lieth the seed. Of this cotton, or
whatsoever it be, good beds may be made, more excellent a thousand times than of
feathers, and softer than common cotton. We have sowed of the said seed, or grain, in
divers places of Paris, but it did not prove.
Marc Lescarbot / History of New France 1609

IT COMES UP in the month of May, much like asparagus; and when it is nine or ten
inches high, is cut down, sold at market, dressed and eaten much in the same manner ...
In the month of August there is an abundant dew upon its leaves and flowers, which
continues for a fortnight or three weeks. This being shaken off into basons before or
immediately after sun-rise, a quantity of sweet liquor or syrup is collected, which being
boiled down to a proper consistency, yields a very good sugar resembling honey both in
colour and flavour. Some of the Canadian farmers procure a tolerable quantity of this
sugar for their family use; but very little is ever sold ... The pods ... [when ripe] contain a
fine white silky substance, extremely soft, and resembling cotton ... The Canadians
make no other use of the cotton than as a substitute for feathers to fill their mattresses
and pillows with ... Were I to reside in Canada, there is nothing in which I should more
delight than in forming a large plantation of the *cotonnier*.
John Lambert / Travels 1810

Mosses or Lichens

All lichens consist of a symbiosis of fungi and algae, with the form of the plant determined by the fungal partner.

REINDEER LICHENS / *Cladonia rangiferina* are species of *Cladonia*, belonging to the subsection *Cladina*, and are intricately branched, grey lichens. They grow on the ground and are grazed by caribou. (Illustrated)

Other lichens grow on trees in areas with high rainfall. Many are long and thread-like, hanging from branches of the trees.

THE REINDEER MOSS (*Lichen rangiferinus*) grows plentifully in the woods around Quebec. M. Gauthier, and several other gentlemen, told me that the French, on their long journeys through the woods, on account of their fur trade with the Indians, sometimes boil this moss and drink the decoction for want of better food, when their provisions are at an end, and they say it is very nutritive. Several Frenchmen who have been in the Terra Labrador, where there are many reindeer (which the French and Indians here call cariboux), related that all the land there is in most places covered with this reindeer moss, so that the ground looks white as snow.

Peter Kalm / Travels into North America 1753–61

THE NEXT DAY we came to ten lodges of Kootenay and Lake Indians; they had nothing to give us but a few dried carp and some moss bread. This is made of a fine black moss, found on the west side of the mountains attached to the bark of a resinous rough barked fir and also the larch. It is about six inches in length, nearly as fine as the hair of the head; it is washed, beaten, and then baked, when it becomes a cake of black bread, of a slight bitter taste, but acceptable to the hungry, and in hard times of great service to the Indians. I never could relish it; it has just nourishment enough to keep a person alive.

David Thompson / Travels in Western North America 1784–1812

IN THE WOODS from York here, I looked very particularly for the Moss on trees by which the Indians are said to find the points of the Compass. It is the green moss similar to that which grows among our grass & tho' not plentiful is seldom to be sought far – It is said to grow on the North side of Trees – but I saw it on all sides – the trees which grow perfectly upright seldom have any except small tufts on projecting boughs, those which have a bend are covered with moss on the upper side which ever direction that lies in – sometimes a tree which is crooked or branches different ways will have moss to several different points – It appears therefore to be a very uncertain mark – All that can be said is that perhaps an upright tree is more apt to have tufts on the North side than any other – and perhaps a slighter bend from the North will give a closer coat of Moss, than an equal bend from any other point. – Every person who may have occasion to be in the woods ought to carry his compass as regularly as his watch. –

Lord Selkirk / Diary 1803–4

Nettle

Nettle Family / Urticaceae

STINGING NETTLE / *Urtica dioica*
Now thought to be the aggregate species across Canada and the United States, perhaps with introductions in some places.
Distinguishing features stem and leaf stalks densely beset with stinging hairs, flowers in branched clusters. Found in waste places.

There is also an introduced species, *Urtica urens*, Dog Nettle or Burning Nettle, which occurs from British Columbia to Prince Edward Island.

The illustration is of the Wood Nettle / *Urtica gracilis*.

The fibre of the nettle yields a yarn, said to be superior to jute and hemp, though inferior to flax. In spring the leaves are sometimes boiled and eaten.

Urtication, or rubbing with nettles, is said to have been used for treating rheumatism right up to the present century.

THERE WERE also several women [Hiroquois] who were gathering the hemp of the country, that is, nettles, of which they make very strong ropes.
Paul Le Jeune / Jesuit Relations 1636

THE CARRIERS [who live west of the Rocky Mountains] make canoes, which are clumsily wrought, of the aspin tree, as well as of the bark of the spruce fir ... The women make excellent nets, of the inner bark of the willow tree, and of nettles, which answer better for taking small fish, than any which we obtain from Canada, made of twine or thread.
Daniel Williams Harmon / A Journal of Voyages and Travels 1820

WE STUMBLED upon a brook, running merrily over a gravelly bottom, the mouth of which is imperceptible from the lake. Where it comes from and whether it may not be another mouth of the former one I cannot tell, for the ground was covered with a kind of nettle, growing very high, which, though not so painful as our English nettle, made nothing of stinging through our trousers.
John Langton / Letters 1833–7

Oak

Beech Family / Fagaceae

There are about 75 or 80 species of oak which are native to North America, mostly to southern Ontario and the United States.

RED OAK / *Quercus rubra*
Also called Northern Red Oak; Black Oak; Champion Oak; Spanish Oak.
Distinguishing features a large forest tree with lobed leaves, the lobes triangular and tipped by bristles. Found, often in sandy soil, Prince Edward Island to southern Ontario, and south.

Acorns ripe October to November. The wood is hard, heavy, strong, and coarse-grained.

Bur or Mossy-cup Oak / *Quercus macrocarpa* grows farther north and west than any of the other eastern oaks (to eastern Saskatchewan). Garry or Oregon Oak / *Quercus garryana* is the only species of oak native to British Columbia.

The illustration is of the White Oak / *Quercus alba*.

[BRÉBEUF and Lalemant have been murdered and the surviving priests and Hurons are starving.] Their ordinary food is now nothing but acorns, or a certain bitter root which they name *otsa*; and yet, fortunate is he who can have any of these. Those who have none, live partly on garlic baked under the ashes, or cooked in water, without other sauce … Our Fathers [are] unable to forsake them … In this service, acorns and exceedingly bitter roots seem to them a dish more delicious than the daintiest morsels of Europe.

Paul Ragueneau / Jesuit Relations 1649

SEVERAL PLACES of *Acadia* afford Masts as strong as those we have from *Norway*; and if there were occasion, all sorts of Ships might be built there: For if you'll believe the Carpenters, the Oak of that Country is better than ours in *Europe*.

Baron de Lahontan / New Voyages to North-America 1703

THERE IS ANOTHER article of food made use of amongst … the Chinook Indians … The whites have given it the name of Chinook olives, and it is prepared as follows: – About a bushel of acorns are placed in a hole dug for the purpose close to the entrance of the lodge or hut, covered over with a thin layer of grass, on the top of which is laid about half a foot of earth. Every member of the family henceforth regards this hole as the special place of deposit for his urine, which is on no occasion to be diverted from its legitimate receptacle. In this hole the acorns are allowed to remain four or five months before they are considered fit for use … the product is regarded by them as the greatest of all delicacies.

Paul Kane / Wanderings of an Artist 1859

Pine

Pine Family, Conifers / Pinaceae

There are about 35 species of pine in North America, 9 of which are native to Canada. SOFT PINES: Eastern White Pine, Western White Pine, Whitebark Pine, Limber Pine. *Distinguishing features* leaves are in bunches of 5, cone scales are relatively thin, and the wood is generally soft and workable.

HARD PINES: Red Pine, Jack Pine (illustrated), Pitch Pine, Ponderosa Pine, Shore Pine, Lodgepole Pine. *Distinguishing features* leaves in bunches of 2 or 3, scales thicker, wood harder.

THE INHABITANTS [of Baie St Paul] chiefly live by agriculture, and the profits arising from their commerce in tar, which they extract from the red pine, by making an incision into the tree in the spring of the year, when the sap is rising, and before the tree has stopped running, it will produce several gallons of turpentine, which they easily manufacture into tar.

ON MY FIRST ARRIVAL in this country, I was struck with the loftiness of the pines, fir-trees, and cedars, which are of a size perfectly astonishing. There are two sorts of pine, both of them yielding turpentine. The white pines produce, on their upper extremities a kind of mushroom, which the Canadians administer in cases of the dysentery.
Thomas Anburey / Travels 1789 (both passages)

WE WENT TO SEE two of the *voyageurs* launch the canoe for the purpose of fire-fishing. This sport is pursued by placing over the bow a bundle of bark, pine-knots full of turpentine, or other combustible wood, and then paddling slowly over the water. One man paddles, whilst the other kneels near the fire, and watching the fish as they rise to scan the strange appearance which attracts them, he, with unerring aim, darts his fish-spear into 'the victim of curiosity.'

The sight of the canoes fishing by fire light is very beautiful on a dark summer night. Large sparkles are continually falling, and floating like meteors on the placid bosom of the dark lake; whilst the fitful blazing of the fire, the strong reflections on the dark figures in the canoe, and the stream of pencilled light which follows its wake between the observer and the shore, heighten the truly picturesque scene.
Sir Richard Henry Bonnycastle / The Canadas in 1841

Pitcher Plant

Pitcher Plant Family / Sarraceniaceae

Sarracenia purpurea
Also called Petits cochons; Herbe-crapaud;
Side-saddle Flower; Huntsman's-cup; Indian
Cup or Pitcher; Adam's-cup; Whippoorwill's-
boots; Skunk-cabbage; Watches; Small-pox
Plant; Fly-trap; Meadow- or Fever-cup.
Distinguishing features leaves large and
pitcher-like; flowers deep purple, nodding, al-
most spherical.

Found in peat bogs, Labrador, Newfoundland to northeastern British Columbia and
south.

The Family *Sarraceniaceae* consists of three
genera and about ten species, all natives of
America.

The Pitcher Plant is the floral emblem of
Newfoundland.

THERE IS a curious aquatic plant that grows in shallow, stagnant, or slow-flowing
waters; it will contain a full wine-glass of water. A poor soldier brought it to me, and told
me it resembled a plant he used to see in Egypt, that the soldiers called the 'Soldier's
drinking-cup'; and 'many a good draught of pure water,' he said, 'I have drank from
them.'

Another specimen was presented me by a gentleman who knew my predilection for
strange plants; he very aptly gave it the name of 'Pitcher-plant'; it very probably belongs
to the tribe that bear that name.

Catharine Parr Traill / The Backwoods of Canada 1836

BUT OF ALL THE natural productions of the swamps none is more singular than the
water-bearer, pitcher-plant, or side-saddle flower, Sarracenia purpurea, so named after
Dr. Sarrazin of Quebec, which is an herbaceous perennial. Its leaves are tubular or
pitcher-shaped, and are always filled with about a wine glassful of the purest water, in
which many insects find a grave, and as the receptacles are lined with inverted hairs,
preventing escape, it is probable that these insects contribute to the food of the plant.*
The flower is purple, large, and handsome.
* Anspach observes that the flower, shaped like a lady's saddle, is surrounded with a vast
number of pitchers, the lids of which expand or shut according to the necessities of the
plant &c.; these pitchers are of so strong a texture that they bear heat enough for some
minutes to boil the water in them.

Sir Richard Henry Bonnycastle / Newfoundland in 1842

Plantain

Plants belonging to three distinct families are called plantain. The most widely distributed, Plantaginaceae, consists of a number of species including:

COMMON PLANTAIN / *Plantago major* (illustrated)

Also called Grand Plantain; Dooryard Plantain; Way-side or Round-leaf Plantain; Broadleaf; Hen-plant; Lamb's-foot; Way-bread; Healing-blade; Whiteman's-foot.

Distinguishing features a common weed with broad basal leaves and a long dense flower spike.

Found in waste places, nearly throughout North America. May to September. It is an introduced weed. Buckthorn / *Plantago lanceolata*, etc, are similar.

The quote may refer to Pale Indian Plantain / *Cacalia atriplicifolia* or a related species. These plantains belong to the Composite Family and are said to have medicinal value. There are records of this plantain occurring in Canada, probably based on a similar plant such as *Prenanthes*.

The various Rattlesnake Plantains, e.g., *Goodyera repens*, belong to the Orchis Family. They are so named because their leaves resemble the skin of the rattlesnake.

THE SCALES of these rattle-snakes are of variegated colours, and extremely beautiful, the head is small, with a very quick and piercing eye; their flesh, notwithstanding the venom they are possessed of, is very delicious, far superior to that of an eel, and produces a very rich soup.

The bite of these reptiles is certain death, unless proper remedies are applied. Providence has been so attentive to our preservation ... that near to where these reptiles resort, there grows a plant with a large broad leaf, called *plantain*, which being bruised and applied to the wound, is a sure antidote to the ill effects of its venom.

The virtues of this plant were discovered by a negro in Virginia, for which he obtained his liberty and a pension for life.

This discovery, like many others equally surprizing, was the mere effect of chance. This poor negro, having been bit by one of these snakes in the leg, it swelled in an instant to such a degree, that he was unable to walk; lying down on the grass in great anguish, he gathered some of this plant, and chewing it, applied it to the wound, imagining it would cool the inflammation; this giving him instant relief, he renewed the application several times, and the swelling abated, so as to enable him to walk home to his master's plantation; after repeating the same for the space of two or three days, he was perfectly recovered.

Thomas Anburey / Travels 1789

Plum

Rose Family / Rosaceae

Two wild plums are native to parts of Canada and the United States.

AMERICAN PLUM / *Prunus americana*
Also called Wild Yellow or Red Plum; Horse-, Hog's-, or Goose-plum.
Distinguishing features alternate oval leaves; white flowers turning to pink; twigs develop coarse spurs which distinguish them from any of the closely related cherries.

Fruit ripe August to October. Found Quebec to southern Saskatchewan, and south.

CANADA PLUM / *Prunus nigra* (illustrated)
Also called Red Plum; Horse Plum.

Similar to the American Plum but has broader leaves.

Nova Scotia to southeastern Manitoba, and south.

ON THE TWENTY-SIXTH of the same month of August, some Savages who were passing our House showed us some plums they had gathered in the woods not far from there; they were as large as the little apricots of France, their stone being flat like that of the apricot. This leads me to say that the cold of these Countries does not prevent fruit from growing. We shall know from experience, in a few years, for we have grafted some cuttings which have started very well.

Paul Le Jeune / Jesuit Relations 1634–6

AT THE HEAD of Lake St François, we landed on a small island, called 'Isle aux Raisins,' on account of the number of wild vines growing upon it. The bateaux men gathered great quantities of the grapes, wherewith the trees were loaded, and also an abundance of plums, which they devoured with great avidity. Neither of the fruits, however, were very tempting to persons whose palates had been accustomed to the taste of garden fruits. The grapes were sour, and not larger than peas; and as for the plums, though much larger in size, yet their taste did not differ materially from that of sloes.

Isaac Weld / Travels through North America 1799

THE NATIVE PLUMS are not very good in their raw state, but they make an excellent preserve, and good wine.

Samuel Strickland / Twenty-Seven Years in Canada West 1853

Poison Ivy

Cashew Family / Anacardiaceae

Rhus radicans
Also called Herbe à la puce; Climbing or
Three-leaved Ivy; Poison Oak; Climath;
Trailing or Climbing Sumac; Mercury; Black
Mercury-vine; Markry; Mark-weed; Picry.
Distinguishing features each leaf composed of
three leaflets, often drooping. Many variations.
   Found in woods and waste places almost
throughout North America.

ONE OF MY GUIDES lately made a trial of the virtue of an herb which is to be met with every where, and the knowledge of which is exceeding necessary to travellers, not for any good qualities it possesses, for I have never as yet heard any attributed to it, but because too much care cannot be taken to avoid it; this is called, *L'herbe a la puce*, or Flea-wort, but this name is not expressive enough to show the effects it produces. These are more or less sensible according to the constitution of those it happens to touch; there are even some persons on whom it does not operate at all; but some persons merely by looking upon it are seized with a violent fever, which lasts more than fifteen days, and is accompanied with a very troublesome scab, attended with a prodigious itching all over the body; it operates on others only when they touch it, and then the patient appears as if entirely covered over with a leprosy: and some have been known to have had their hands quite spoiled with it. No remedy is as yet known for it but patience; after some time it goes entirely off.

Pierre-François-Xavier de Charlevoix / Journal of a Voyage 1744

17TH OCTOBER 1847
A very strange thing happened to us all during the summer. Frederick, during the haying season, poisoned himself in the legs and feet, due to touching what they call here 'poison ivy.' It was six weeks before he could wear his boots, and even now he is not free from lameness. Eliza, myself, and the baby are now suffering. It first shows itself by a small white pimple, increasing to that of a half crown. It discharges all the time, and is very painful. I am now writing sitting on the bed, for I am not able to put my legs to the floor without great pain.

   Later: We have all recovered from our poisonous sores. I cannot tell you more about the poison ivy as very little is known. It is by contact with the plant that the damage is done, though there have been instances of contact with a sufferer passing it on. Remedies vary and do little good, and all are external. The poison gets into the blood and only time purifies it and makes a cure.

George Stacey / The Stacey Letters 1836–58

Prickly Pear Cactus

Cactus Family / Cactaceae

MANY-SPINED OPUNTIA / *Opuntia polyacantha*
Also called Tuna.
Distinguishing features remarkable yellow flower; pale green pads with many fine bristles. Fruit dry, very prickly. Found in dry sandy soil, southern Saskatchewan to southern British Columbia, and south.
  Western Prickly Pear Cactus / *Opuntia compressa* (illustrated) is similar and is found in southern Ontario.

[ON THE BANKS of the Red Deer river] The men are also busily employed making arrows – of the Sascuttem wood, which is very hard ... there is great plenty of it here along the river under the Bank. I found on this side near the top of the Bank – a particular kind of Grass – very full of sharp Prickles of 2 Inches long & the thickness of a Pin – which grew upon a wrinkled round flatt knob of 1½ Inch diamiter, the outer Skin has much the appearance of a Cucumber – & are cennected together in the following manner ∞∞∞ some has 8 or 10 of these going together & a single root only found under one at the end. They are very bad to walk amongst – runny immediately thro the shoes usally worn here of dressd leather – the Indians say that far to the Southward, about & beyond the Mis sis su ry river, the ground is almost covered with them for a great distance & so very large – & form large bushes that at a Distance they have often been taken for Buffalo laid down – when on their war excursions – in these parts – the only method they have to fortify their feet against these formidable & very bad things, they make shoes of the raw hide of the Buffalo – which the prickles are not strong enough to penetrate thro!
  Peter Fidler / Journal 1792–3

Raspberry

Rose Family / Rosaceae

The genus Rubus includes Raspberries and Blackberries. Species are widely distributed across North America.
RED RASPBERRY / *Rubus idaeus* (illustrated) Found in dry or rocky soil, Labrador, New-foundland to British Columbia, and south. One of the most common species.

BLACKBERRY / *Rubus occidentalis* Also called Black Raspberry; Thimble-berry; Black-cap; Scotch-cap; Purple Raspberry. British Columbia, Ontario to New Brunswick.

AT THE ENTRANCE [to the harbour of La Have], on the left, there is an island which is called Isle aux Framboises … its top being nothing but raspberry bushes. In the spring it is all covered with Pigeons which go there to eat the berries.
  Nicolas Denys / Description and Natural History 1672

MY HEALTH being at length re-established and my wound healed … I accordingly commenced a regular diary … I at length succeeded in obtaining a very tolerable ink, by boiling the juice of the black-berry with a mixture of finely powdered charcoal and filtering it through a cloth … As for quills I found no difficulty in procuring them, whenever I wanted, from the crows and ravens with which the beach was almost always covered, attracted by the offal of whales, seals &c which were so tame that I could easily kill them with stones, while a large clam shell furnished me with an ink stand.
  John R. Jewitt / Narrative 1803–5

THIS LITTLE LAKE lies in the heart of the wilderness. There is but one clearing upon its shores, and that had been made by lumberers many years before; the place abounded with red cedar. A second growth of young timber had grown up in this spot, which was covered also with raspberry-bushes – several hundred acres being entirely overgrown with this delicious berry.
  It was here annually that we used to come in large picnic parties, to collect this valuable fruit for our winter preserves, in defiance of black flies, mosquitoes, snakes, and even bears; all which have been encountered by berry-pickers upon this spot, as busy and as active as themselves, gathering an ample repast from Nature's bounteous lap.
  Susanna Moodie / Roughing it in the Bush 1852

THEY GROW more plentifully in the angles of the snake-fences in Canada than blackberries do in England. They are a delicious fruit, and particularly grateful in a hot day to the weary traveller.
  Samuel Strickland / Twenty-Seven Years in Canada West 1853

Rice

Grass Family / Gramineae

WILD RICE / *Zizania aquatica*
Also called Indian Rice; Water Oats; Riz sauvage; Folle avoine; Canada-rice; Water-rice. *Distinguishing features* tall, aquatic grass with long flat leaf-blades.

Various forms are found in swamps from New Brunswick to Saskatchewan and south. June to October. The plant's range is thought to have been increased by planting for duck food.

WITH ALL THESE PRECAUTIONS, we joyfully plied our paddles on a portion of Lake Huron, on that of the Ilinois and the Bay des Puants.

The first nation that we came to was that of the Folle Avoine … The wild oat, whose name they bear because it is found in their country, is a sort of grass … In the month of September … they go in canoes through these fields of wild oats; they shake its ears into the canoe, on both sides, as they pass through. The grain falls out easily, if it be ripe, and they obtain their supply in a short time. But, in order to clean it from the straw and to remove it from a husk in which it is enclosed, they dry it in the smoke, upon a wooden grating, under which they maintain a slow fire for some days. When the oats are thoroughly dry, they put them in a skin made into a bag, thrust it into a hole dug in the ground for this purpose, and tread it with their feet – so long and so vigorously that the grain separates from the straw, and is very easily winnowed. After this, they pound it to reduce it to flour, or even, without pounding it, they boil it in water, and season it with fat.
Louis Jolliet and Jacques Marquette / The Mississippi Voyage 1673

[IN THE GREAT LAKES AREA the Indians] have another Resois [resource] – the Bottom of the Bay Produces a Large Quantity of Wilde Rice which thay Geather in Sept for food … This Grane Looks in its Groth & Stock & Ears Like Ry and the Grane is of the same Culler But Longer and Slimer. When it is Cleaned fit for youse thay Baile it as we Due Rise and Eat it with Bairs Greas and Suger But the Greas thay ad as it is Bileing which helps to Soffen it and make it Brake in the same Maner as Rise. When thay take it out of thare Cettels for yous thay ad a Little suger and is Eaten with fresh Vensen or fowls.
Peter Pond / Narrative 1775–82

IN THE MONTH OF September the Indians bring wild rice to Kingston, which grows on the borders of the lake, especially on the American side. This plant, which loves marshy ground, succeeds there remarkably well. The Indians bring yearly from four to five hundred pounds of this rice, which several inhabitants of Kingston purchase for their own consumption. This rice is of a smaller and darker grain that that, which comes from Carolina, Egypt, etc., but grows as white in the water, is of as good a flavor, and affords full as good nourishment, as the latter. The culture of rice would be very useful in Europe for the subsistence of the poor, especially as in those parts the frequent use of it would not prove injurious to health, which it certainly does in hot countries.
François la Rochefoucault-Liancourt / Travels 1799

THE DUCKS are in the finest order during the early part of the summer, when they resort to the rice-beds in vast numbers, getting very fat on the green rice, which they eagerly devour.
Catharine Parr Traill / The Backwoods of Canada 1836

Rose

Rose Family / Rosaceae

WILD ROSE
Familiar shrubs or vines, easily recognized by
their simple but showy five-petalled flowers.

Pasture Rose / *Rosa virginiana* is one of the
commonest. Woods' Rose / *Rosa woodsii* is a
prairie rose. Nootka Rose / *Rosa nutkana* is
widely distributed in British Columbia, southern Alaska, California, south. Sweetbrier /
Rosa eglanteria is naturalized from Europe.
Called 'Eglantine' by Chaucer, Spenser, and
Shakespeare.

The Wild Rose is the floral emblem of Alberta, Georgia, Iowa, and North Dakota.

The illustration shows the Meadow Rose /
Rosa blanda.

I CAN ASSERT that on the fifteenth of June there were wild roses here [Hudson Bay],
as beautiful and fragrant as those at Quebec. The season seemed to me farther advanced,
the air extremely mild and agreeable. There was no night during my visit; the twilight
had not yet faded from the west when the dawn of day appeared in the East.

Charles Albanel / Jesuit Relations 1671–2

FEBRUARY 22, Wednesday. *Lac la Pêche or Fishing Lake* [on the Qu'Appelle River],
which lies about two Days march out into the Plain from Alexandria, which place I left on
the 15th Ult. accompanied by a dozen of our people and am come to pass the remainder of
the Winter here along side of the x.y. People ... For some time after our arrival we
subsisted on *Rose-buds*! which we gathered in the fields, but they are neither very
nourishing nor palatable, yet they are much better than nothing at all, but where to
procure anything better I knew not, for the Buffaloe at that time were a great distance out
into the Plains.

Daniel Williams Harmon / Journal of Voyages and Travels 1820

Saskatoon

Rose Family / Rosaceae

Amelanchier alnifolia
Also called Serviceberry; Petites poires; Indian
Pear; Shadbush; Siwash Berry; Pigeon-berry.
   The Saskatoon is a western species of Service-
berry; it also grows in Ontario and western
Quebec. Similar species grow in various parts of
North America.
   They are deciduous shrubs or small trees
with simple alternate leaves and white flowers
in spring; small sweet berry-like fruit ripens
June to July.

THIS SHRUB is common as far north as lat. 62'. It abounds on the sandy plains of the
Saskatchewan ... Its berries, about the size of a pea, are the finest fruit in the country,
and are used by the Crees ... both in a fresh and dried state. They form a pleasant addition
to pemmican, and make excellent puddings, very little inferior to plum-puddings.
   John Richardson / Franklin: Narrative of a Journey 1823

HAD 'BERRY-PEMMICAN' at supper. That is to say, the ordinary buffalo pemmican,
with Saskootoom berries sprinkled through it at the time of making, – which acts as
currant jelly does with venison, correcting the greasiness of the fat by a slightly acid
sweetness. Sometimes wild cherries are used instead of the Meesasskootoom-meena.
Berry-pemmican is usually the best of its kind, but poor is the best. Take scrapings from
the driest outside corner of a very stale piece of cold roast beef, add to it lumps of tallowy
rancid fat, then garnish all with long human hairs (on which string pieces, like beads,
upon a necklace), and short hairs of oxen, or dogs, or both, – and you have a fair
imitation of common pemmican, though I should rather suppose it to be less nasty.
   Pemmican is most endurable when uncooked. My men used to fry it with grease,
sometimes stirring-in flour, and making a flabby mess, called 'rubaboo', which I found
almost uneatable. Carefully-made pemmican, such as that flavoured with the Saskootoom berries, or some that we got from the mission at St. Ann, or the sheep-pemmican
given us by the Rocky Mountain hunters, is nearly good, – but, in two senses, a little of
it goes a long way.
   The Earl of Southesk / Saskatchewan and the Rocky Mountains 1859–60

Sassafras

Laurel Family / Lauraceae

SASSAFRAS / *Sassafras albidum*
Also called Ague Tree; Universal Tree;
Cinnamon-wood; Smelling-stick.
Distinguishing features a medium-sized tree;
leaves often mitten-shaped or three-lobed and
aromatic; bark rough and aromatic.

Found in dry or sandy soil, Maine to southern Ontario, Michigan, Iowa, Florida, and
Texas. Flowers April to May. Red berry-like
fruit ripe July to August.

In the past every part of the tree has been
used medicinally. The bark affords a dye for a
handsome and permanent orange colour. The
oil of sassafras used in soap and perfumes comes
from this tree.

The Sassafras Fergusson refers to is probably
the North American Pawpaw / *Asimina triloba*,
also called Custard-apple. This shrub or small
tree produces a sweet pendulous brown (when
ripe) fruit. Found in rich woods in southern
Ontario and south.

A TREE having leaves like to oak-leaves, but less jagged, whose wood is of very good
scent and most excellent for the curing of many diseases, as the pox and the sickness of
Canada, which I call *pthisis*.
  Marc Lescarbot / History of New France 1609

BUT THE MOST COMMON and most wonderful plant in those countries [of the
Iroquois] is that which we call the universal plant, because its leaves, when pounded, heal
in a short time wounds of all kinds; these leaves, which are as broad as one's hand, have
the shape of a lily as depicted in heraldry; and its roots have the smell of the laurel. The
most vivid scarlet, the brightest green, the most natural yellow and orange of Europe
pale before the various colours that our Savages procure from roots. I say nothing of trees
as tall as oaks, whose leaves are as large and as open as those of cabbages; or of many
other plants, peculiar to this country, because as yet we are ignorant of their properties.
  Paul Le Jeune / Jesuit Relations 1656–7

BY ONE OF THEM [the few physicians] I was informed that the inferior classes of the
inhabitants [of the Lake Huron area] dread their advice in intermittent fevers, because
they always prescribe bark; and that poor people, instead of following their advice, have
recourse to a sort of magic charm, in which universal confidence is placed in this country.
If seized with the ague, they go into the forest, search out a branch of an elm or sassafras,
of the last year's growth; fasten to this branch, without breaking it off the tree, a thread,
which must not be quite new; tie as many knots, as they think they shall have fits of the
fever; and then return home, perfectly convinced, that they shall not experience more
fits, than they have bound themselves to sustain, by the number of knots they have tied.
The first discoverers of this arcanum used to make so few knots, that the ague would
frequently disappoint their hopes, but they who at present practice this superstition tie so
many, that the febrile matter is generally carried off, before the number of fits comes up
to that of the knots.
  François la Rochefoucault-Liancourt / Travels 1799

THE UNDERGROWTH, or shrubbery, consists of sassafras, with a bud in taste resembling a custard.
  Adam Fergusson / Practical Notes 1831

Spruce

Pine Family, Conifers / Pinaceae

Five species of spruces (and two varieties) are native to Canada. The Red Spruce is found only in eastern Canada and the United States. The Sitka and Engelmann spruces are western. The White and the Black Spruce grow in almost every part of Canada and in parts of the United States.

'Spruce beer' was made from both the eastern Red Spruce and the wide-ranging Black Spruce.

Red Spruce / *Picea rubens* is a slender tree with reddish bark and bright yellow-green foliage; oval cones in autumn. Sometimes called Yellow Spruce.

Black Spruce / *Picea mariana* has blue-green foliage.

The illustration shows the White Spruce / *Picea canadensis*

THE SOLDIERS, not only at the *Isle au Noix*, but likewise at St John's, have been very subject to the scurvy, not having any other than salt provisions, but by drinking plentifully of spruce beer, they are now all in perfect health, which clearly proves that liquor to be a powerful antiscorbutic. It is so much known in England, as to need no description; the only difference between the spruce there and here is, that here it is made with the branches of the tree itself, and there with the essence.

Thomas Anburey / Travels 1789

WHEN BOTTLED and kept, this liquor forms a very pleasant summer drink, but the European palate requires to be accustomed to it. There can be no doubt that it is highly salutary to persons living so much on salt fish as the farmers and fishermen here do, and no respectable farm-house should ever be without it, the only expense being that of the molasses and the time required to make the beverage. About ten gallons of good spruce beer may be manufactured for half a dollar, or a little more than two shillings.

Sir Richard Henry Bonnycastle / Newfoundland in 1842

Strawberry

Rose Family / Rosaceae

WILD STRAWBERRY
Two widely distributed species are the Common or Scarlet Strawberry / *Fragaria virginiana* (illustrated) and the Woodland Strawberry / *Fragaria vesca*.

[A FRIGHTFUL EPIDEMIC is laying waste the Huron Indians. They turn against the Jesuits and resort to devil cures]: those demons ... said to Tsondacouané, 'thou art now safe; we can do nothing more to thee ... we must reveal to thee our food, which is nothing more than clear soup with strawberries.' There was much probability of their finding strawberries in the month of January! But our Savages keep dried ones, and they vied with one another in eating them, in order not to be sick.
   François-Joseph Le Mercier / Jesuit Relations 1637

'TIS AMAZINGLY PLEASING to see the strawberries and wild pansies peeping their little foolish heads from beneath the snow.
Frances Brooke / The History of Emily Montague 1769

IN MAY, the weather became uncommonly mild and pleasant, and so forward was vegetation that I picked a plenty of strawberries by the middle of the month. Of this fruit there are great quantities on this coast, and I found them a most delicious treat [west coast of Vancouver Island].
   John R. Jewitt / Narrative 1803–5

THE STRAWBERRY, called by the Crees otei-meena, or heart-berry, is found in abundance [in the neighbourhood of Cumberland House].
   Sir John Franklin / Narrative of a Journey 1823

Sumac

Cashew Family / Anacardiaceae

SCARLET SUMAC / *Rhus glabra*
Also called Smooth Upland Sumac; Vinegar-
tree; Senhalanac; Shoe-make.
Distinguishing features flaming scarlet or yel-
low leaves in autumn; clusters of greenish-
yellow flowers become reddish densely-hairy
fruits.
   Found in dry soil, Quebec to Saskatchewan,
British Columbia, and in the United States.
   The foliage is sometimes used for tanning.
Two closely related species are Staghorn Su-
mac / *Rhus typhina* (illustrated) and Dwarf,
Shining, or Wingrib Sumac / *Rhus copallina*.

THE INDIANS smoke the bark of many different trees, and a great variety of herbs and
leaves besides tobacco. The most agreeable of any of these substances which they smoke
are the leaves of the sumach tree, rhus-toxicodendron. This is a graceful shrub, which
bears leaves somewhat similar to those of the ash. Towards the latter end of autumn they
turn of a bright red colour, and when wanted for smoking are plucked off and dried in the
sun. Whilst burning they afford a very agreeable perfume. These leaves are very
commonly smoked, mixed with tobacco, by the white people of the country; the smoke
of them by themselves alone is said to be prejudicial to the lungs. The sumach tree bears
tufted bunches of crimson flowers. One of these bunches dipped lightly, for a few times,
into a bowl of punch, gives the liquor a very agreeable acid, and in the southern states it is
common to use them for that purpose, but it is a dangerous custom, as the acid, though
extremely agreeable to the palate, is of a poisonous quality, and never fails to produce a
most alarming effect on the bowels if used too freely.
   Isaac Weld / Travels through North America 1799

THE INNER BARK of the root of the sumach, roasted, and reduced to powder, is a good
remedy for the ague, a tea-spoonful given between the hot and cold fit.
   Susanna Moodie / Roughing it in the Bush 1852

Sunflower

Composite Family / Compositae

There are many species of this familiar plant.
COMMON SUNFLOWER / *Helianthus annuus*
is a garden plant in eastern Canada and the
United States but grows wild on the prairies and
in British Columbia, California, and Texas.
Other species such as *Helianthus strumosus*
and *Helianthus divaricatus* are wild in the east.
JERUSALEM ARTICHOKE / *Helianthus*
tuberosus (illustrated) is a large Sunflower.
Also called Canada Potato and Topinambour.

   Found in moist soil, Prince Edward Island,
Nova Scotia, to Saskatchewan, and south. It is a
garden escape or persists from plantings.

   The name is derived from the Greek: 'helios,'
sun, and 'anthos,' flower.

ANOTHER of their [the Seneca near Geneva, New York] greatest dishes is Indian meal
cooked in water and then served in a wooden bowl with two fingers of bear's grease or oil
of sun-flowers or of butternuts upon it. There was not a child in the village but was eager
to bring us now stalks of Indian corn, at another time squashes, or it might be other small
fruits that they go and gather in the woods.

   François Dollier de Casson and René de Bréhant de Galinée / Journal 1669–70

THE *soleil* is another very common plant in the fields of the Indians, and which rises to
the height of seven or eight feet. Its flower, which is very thick has much the same figure
with that of the marigold, and the seed is disposed in the same manner; the Indians
extract an oil from it by boiling, with which they anoint their hair.

   Pierre-François-Xavier de Charlevoix / Journal of a Voyage 1744

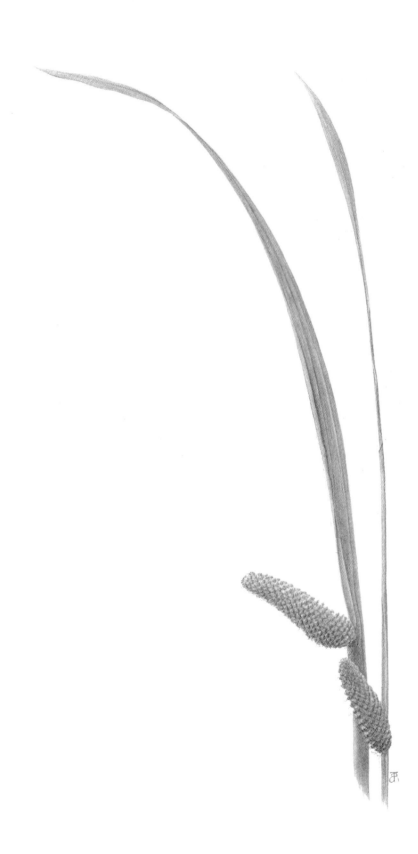

Sweet Flag

Arum Family / Araceae

CALAMUS, SWEET FLAG / *Acorus calamus*
Also called Flag-root; Myrtle-flag or -grass;
Sweet-myrtle; Rédote; Belle-Angélique;
Sedge-grass, -cane, -root, or -rush; Sea-sedge;
Beewort.
Distinguishing features stiff swordlike leaves;
flower-spike juts at an angle from the stem.

Found in wet meadows, swamps, and along
streams, Nova Scotia, Prince Edward Island, to
British Columbia, and south. May to August.

Propagation is by large rootstalks which fur-
nish the drug Calamus. The interior of the stalk
is sweet.

APRIL 24TH, 1794: The Governor has been so ill since the 21st of March that I have not
left his room since that day. He has had such a cough that some nights he could not lie
down, but sat in a chair, total loss of appetite, and such headaches that he could not bear
any person but me to walk across the room or speak loud. There was no medical advice
but that of a horse doctor who pretended to be an apothecary. The Governor, out of
consideration for the convenience of the staff-surgeon, had allowed him to remain at
Niagara ... Capt. Brant's sister prescribed a root – it is, I believe, *calamus*, a genus of
palm, one species of which yields a resin called dragon's blood, the root of which is the
sweet flag – which really relieved his cough in a very short time.

Elizabeth Simcoe / Diary 1792–6

Tobacco

Potato Family / Solanaceae

WILD or INDIAN TOBACCO / *Nicotiana rustica* was and is cultivated by Indians in Canada. It originated in Peru and occurs as a garden escape in southern Ontario and south.

COMMON TOBACCO / *Nicotiana tabacum* (illustrated). Originally from tropical America, it was cultivated in North America from early times. It occurs occasionally as a garden escape in southern Ontario and south.

THE GASPESIANS ... consider, esteem, and regard [tobacco] as a kind of manna which has come to them from Heaven, since Papkootparout gave the first use thereof to the Gaspesian people ... In fact tobacco, which they call *tamahoé*, seems to them absolutely essential to enable them to endure the misfortunes of human life. It diverts them in their voyages, gives them wisdom in their councils, decides upon peace and war; it satisfies their hunger, serving both for drink and food; and when any one is dangerously ill, they still hope to see the sick person again in his original health provided that he can still smoke tobacco, while the contrary is a sure indication that he will die.
  Chrestien Le Clercq / New Relation of Gaspesia 1691

THE CALUMET, or Indian pipe, which is much larger than that the Indians usually smoke, is made of marble, stone, or clay, either red, white, or black, according to the custom of the nation, but the red is mostly esteemed; the length of the handle is about four feet and a half, and made of strong cane, or wood, decorated with feathers of various colours, with a number of twists of female hair interwoven in different forms; the head is finely polished; two wings are fixed to it, which make it in appearance not unlike to Mercury's wand. This calumet is the symbol of peace, and the Savages hold it in such estimation, that a violation of any treaty where it has been introduced, would in their opinion, be attended with the greatest misfortunes.
  John Long / Voyages and Travels 1791

A FRENCH CANADIAN is scarcely ever without a pipe in his mouth ... indeed, so much addicted are the people to smoking, that by the burning of the tobacco in their pipes, they commonly ascertain the distance from one place to another. Such a place, they say, is three pipes off, that is, it is so far off that you may smoke three pipes full of tobacco whilst you go thither.
  Isaac Weld / Travels through North America 1799

I MUST SAY, as I sat smoking my pipe and my face besmeared with tobacco juice to keep at bay the d — d mosquitoes still hovering in clouds around me, that my first impressions of the Youcon were anything but favourable.
  Alexander Hunter Murray / Journal of the Yukon 1847–8

THE ESQUIMAUX, both men and women, are immoderately fond of tobacco, which they smoke differently from other people. The bowl of their pipe is less than half the size of a thimble, and two or three whiffs are all they use on each occasion. This smoke, however, they swallow, which produces a transient intoxication or even unconsciousness, under the influence of which they occasionally fall from their seat. When the process is gone through in an unsteady canoe in the water it is not altogether free from danger.
  Bishop William Bompas / History of the Diocese of Mackenzie River 1888

Trillium

Lily Family / Liliaceae

LARGE-FLOWERED TRILLIUM / *Trillium grandiflorum*
Also called White Trillium; Large-flowered Wake-robin; White Lilies; Bath-flower; Trinity-lily.
Distinguishing features large three-petalled white flowers, turning pink with age.
  Found in rich woods, Quebec, Ontario, and south.
  The Western Wake-Robin / *Trillium ovatum* of British Columbia and south has the same appearance. The similar but smaller Nodding Trillium / *Trillium cernuum* ranges from Newfoundland to Saskatchewan and south.

NATURE has scattered with no niggardly hand these remarkable flowers over hill and dale, wide shrubby plain and shady forest glen. In deep ravines, on rocky islets, the bright snow white blossoms of the Trilliums greet the eye and court the hand to pluck them. The old people in this part of the Province call them by the familiar name of Lily. Thus we have *Asphodel Lilies, Douro Lilies*, &c. In Nova Scotia they are called Moose-flowers, probably from being abundant in the haunts of Moose-Deer. In some of the New England States the Trilliums, white and red, are known as the *Death-flower*, but of the origin of so ominous a name we have no record. We might imagine it to have originated in the use of the flower to deck the coffin or graves of the dead in the olden times.
  Catharine Parr Traill / Canadian Wild Flowers 1868

WE PICNICKED in the valley below the lovely trees. Then we went on to the lake, and it is lovely. The shore is gleaming white sand (*porphyry*, says Mr. H., and it is lovely stuff; I brought a handkerchief full to put in my aquarium). Out of the sand grew blueberry plants. Mr. H. 'whipped off' his shoes and stockings and walked about so along the shore. When we returned our horse had escaped, and the men had to hunt for him. I dug up flower roots with dogged persistency, though the mosquitos and black fly bit me till I rushed madly to the lunch basket, grabbed the butter, smeared my face and hands all over, and – went back to the trilliums!
  Juliana Horatia Ewing / 'Canada Home' 1869

Tripe de Roche

A type of lichen which belongs to the genera
Gyrophora and Umbilicaria. See Mosses and
Lichens.

BEING COME to the place of repose, some did goe along the water side on the rocks and
there exposed ourselves to the rigour of the weather. Upon these rocks we find some
shells, blackish without and the inner part whitish by reason of the heat of the sun and of
the humidity. They are in a maner glued to the rock; so we must gett another stone to
gett them off by scraping them hard. When we thought to have enough [we] went back
again to the Cottages, where the rest weare getting the litle fishes ready with trips [tripe
de roche], gutts and all. The kittle was full with the scraping of the rocks, which soone
after it boyled became like starch, black and clammie and easily to be swallowed. I think if
any bird had lighted upon the excrements of the said stuff, they had stuckt to it as if it
weare glue. In the fields we have gathered severall fruits, as goosberyes, blackberrys,
that in an houre we gathered above a bushell of such sorte, although not as yett full ripe.
We boyled it, and then every one had his share. Heere was daintinesse slighted. The
belly did not permitt us to gett on neither shoos nor stockins, that the better we might
goe over the rocks, which did [make] our feet smart [so] that we came backe.
Pierre-Esprit Radisson / Third Journey 1658–60?

WE WERE FORCED to accustom ourselves to eat a certain moss growing upon the rocks.
It is a sort of shell-shaped leaf which is always covered with caterpillars and spiders; and
which, on being boiled, furnishes an insipid soup, black and viscous, that rather serves to
ward off death than to impart life.
Claude-Jean Allouez / Journey to Lake Superior 1665

THERE IS A black, hard, crumply moss, that grows on the rocks and large stones in those
parts [the Barren Grounds], which is of infinite service to the natives, as it sometimes
furnishes them with a temporary subsistence, when no animal food can be procured.
This moss, when boiled, turns to a gummy consistence, and is more clammy in the
mouth than sago; it may, by adding either moss or water, be made to almost any
consistence. It is so palatable, that all who taste it generally grow fond of it. It is remarkably good and pleasing when used to thicken any kind of broth, but it is generally
most esteemed when boiled in fish-liquor.
Samuel Hearne / A Journey from Prince of Wales's Fort 1795

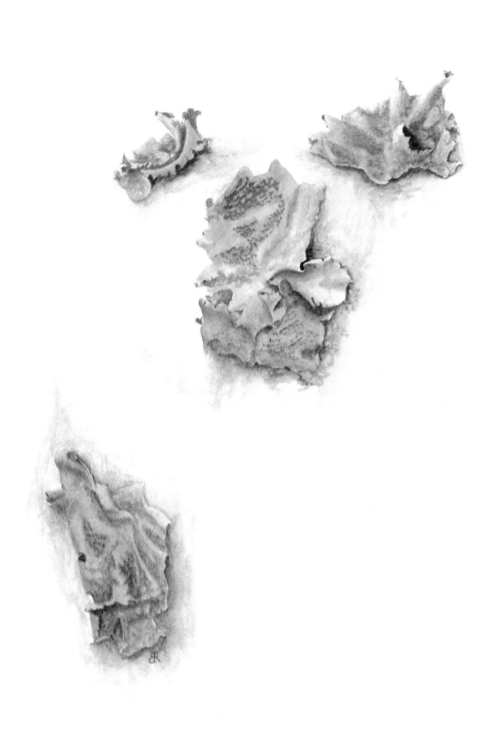

Violet

Violet Family / Violaceae

There are some 200 species of Violaceae, widely
distributed. They are low-growing plants
whose flowers have five petals, distinctively
arranged. The garden pansy belongs to the
Violet Family.

   The illustration shows the Northern White
Violet / *Viola pallens*, the Northern Bog or
Purple Violet / *Viola nephrophylla*, and the
Downy Yellow Violet / *Viola pubescens*.

   The purple Violet is the floral emblem of
New Brunswick.

THE LAND IS, in situation, goodnesse, and fairenes, like the other … but not so sweete,
because the countrey is more northerly and cold. Wee sawe in this Countrey many Vines
growing naturally, which growing up take hold of the trees as they do in Lombardie …
We found also roses, violettes, lillies, and many sorts of herbes and sweete and odorifer-
ous flowers, different from ours.

   Giovanni da Verrazzano / Relation of John Verarzanus 1524

OF VIOLETS we have every variety of colour, size, and shape, lacking only the delightful *viola odorata* of our home woodlands; yet I know not why we should quarrel with
these meek daughters of the spring, because they want the fragrance of their more
favoured sisters.

   Catharine Parr Traill / The Backwoods of Canada 1836

Walnut

Walnut Family / Juglandaceae

Of the six species native to North America the most familiar are the Black Walnut and the Butternut.

BLACK WALNUT / *Juglans nigra*, also called American Walnut, is a valuable tree; it has aromatic compound leaves, scaly bark, and a sweet edible nut. Found in rich soil, southern Ontario to Massachusetts and south.

BUTTERNUT / *Juglans cinerea*, also called White Walnut, Lemon Walnut, and Oil-nut. Similar to the Black Walnut but smaller and less valuable.

HICKORIES belong to the Walnut Family and are often confused with walnuts. The illustration shows the Shagbark Hickory / *Carya ovata*. The Swamp Hickory / *Carya cordiformis* is bitter, and is probably the 'third sort' of nut mentioned by Anburey.

WEE ... ANCHORED about two leagues within the great Riuer which goeth vp to the Sault: In the mouth whereof are thirtie small Ilands, as farre as I could discerne ... which are full of Walnut-trees, which are not much different from ours; and I thinke their Walnuts be good when they bee ripe: I saw many of them vnder the Trees, which were of two sorts, the one small, and the others as long as a mans Thumbe, but they were rotten.

Samuel de Champlain / Voyages and Explorations 1604–16

THERE ARE three sorts of walnuts; the hard, the soft, and another with a thin bark. The hard sort bear a small nut, very good to eat, but apt to occasion costiveness, the wood of which is only fit to burn. The tender bears a large fruit, with a hard shell, the kernels of which are excellent: the wood of this tree is singularly curious, being almost incorruptible in water or in the ground, and difficult to consume in the fire: of this wood the Canadians make their coffins. The third sort produces a nut which is exceedingly bitter, but yields an excellent oil, used by the inhabitants for their lamps.

Thomas Anburey / Travels 1789

MOST OF THE TAVERNS in Upper Canada are indeed a burlesque upon what they profess to be. A tolerable meal can scarcely be procured at any one of them; nay, I have visited several which were not even provided with bread. It is immaterial what meal the traveller calls for, as the same articles will be set before him morning, noon, and night, not even excepting tea, which is considered so essential to comfort; for, if the mistress of the hotel has none of the Chinese plant, she will send one of her children into the woods to gather parts of the evergreen, hemlock, hickory, or other nauseous vegetables, and having made an infusion of the herb brought in, will perhaps inquire of her astonished and shuddering guest, if the tea is sufficiently strong.

John Howison / Sketches of Upper Canada 1821

Wappatoo

Water Plantain Family / Alismataceae

BROAD-LEAVED ARROW-HEAD / *Sagittaria latifolia*
Also called Flèche d'eau; Arrowleaf.
Distinguishing features broad, arrow-shaped leaves; three-petalled white flowers in whorls of three; tuberous root.
   Found growing in shallow water nearly throughout southern Canada and the United States. July to September. Other similar species.

SHELATHWELL RETURNED this evening and brought about 3 Bushells of Potatoes which he gave us. I cannot help mentioning here a circumstance highly to his honour. He had been Poorly and the Doctor gave him medicines which opperated with success. He had scarcely recovered before he set out on this expedition for 'Wapatoes' ... This Chief has ever deserved our warmest Friendship and Praise. His Pacific manners, Truth and honesty are Seldom met with in Savage life.
   Captain Charles Bishop / Journal and Letters 1794–9

THE WAPPATOO is somewhat similar [to camass], but larger, and not so dry or delicate in its flavour.
   Paul Kane / Wanderings of an Artist 1859

Water Lily

Water Lily Family / Nymphaeaceae

YELLOW WATER LILY / *Nuphar advena*
Also called Yellow Pond Lily; Cow Lily; Kelp;
Beaver-root.
   'Nymphaea' from Greek, meaning water-
nymph.
Distinguishing features five or more yellow
sepals, often tinged with red or green, enclose
small stamen-like petals; pad-like leaves.
   Found in ponds and slow streams, southern
Ontario and south. Variations found almost
throughout Canada and the United States. June
to September.
   The root-stalks are sometimes used as a veg-
etable and the seeds in breads and soups.
WHITE WATER LILY / *Nymphaea odorata*
(illustrated)
Also called Fragrant Water-lily; Water
Nymph; Pond Lily; Sweet-scented Water-lily;
Water Cabbage; Nenuphar blanc; Toad-lily.
Distinguishing features familiar round leaves,
numerous waxy-white petals in large flowers.
   Found in ponds, Manitoba to Nova Scotia,
Newfoundland, and south. June to September.

THIS DAY we had a most delightful run among hundreds of islands; sometimes darting
through narrow rocky channels, so narrow that I could not see the water on either side of
the canoe; and then emerging, we glided through vast fields of white water-lilies; it was
perpetual variety, perpetual beauty, perpetual delight and enchantment, from hour to
hour. The men sang their gay French songs, the other canoe joining in the chorus.
   Anna Brownell Jameson / Winter Studies and Summer Rambles 1838

THE GLORIOUS white water-lily, of which we found many specimens about the size of a
small peony, grows often in close conjunction, though not in intermixture, with the
common yellow flower of the same kind.
   Bishop George Mountain / Songs of the Wilderness 1846

Wintergreen

Heath Family / Ericaceae

SPRING WINTERGREEN / *Gaultheria procumbens*
Also called Partridge Berry; Checkerberry; Creeping or Spicy Wintergreen; Chinks; One-berry; Chicken-berry; Red Pollom; Box-, Ground-, Tea-, Green-, Deer-, Hill-, Ivy-, Grouse-, Ginger-, or Spice-berry; Ivory plum; Mountain or Canada Tea; Thé des bois. *Distinguishing features* shiny oval evergreen fragrant leaves; bell-shaped white flowers.

Found in woods and clearings, Nova Scotia and Prince Edward Island to Manitoba, and south. Red berries ripen late in autumn and remain on the plant until spring. Also a western species, Salal / *Gaultheria shallon*.

Other wintergreens such as *Pyrola asarifolia* and *Pyrola grandiflora* belong to the Wintergreen Family.

Mitchella repens is also called Partridgeberry.

HUDSON'S-BAY [is] to the *East*, *Canada* to the *South*; but as for it's Boundaries to the *West* and *North*, they are as yet undiscovered. In the Southern Parts and where we wintered [five miles above York Fort], the Soil is very fertile … There are great variety of Shrubs and Plants … as the Gooseberry, Currant, Craneberry, Shrubs bearing red and black Berries, which the Patridges feed on, therefore called Partridge Berries … Here also are to be met with Strawberries, Angelica, Chickweed, Nettles, Butterflowers, wild Auriculas, Savine, many of the *Lapland* Plants, and others that are unknown to us.
   Henry Ellis / A Voyage to Hudson's-Bay 1746–7

THE PARTRIDGE BERRY (*gaultheria procumbens*) is also abundant. Indeed, the wild and desert solitudes of these regions are amply supplied with the food of birds and of the berry-eating animals; and this amazing fecundity is turned to some account by man, as the berries are now an article of export, both from Labrador and Newfoundland.
   Sir Richard Henry Bonnycastle / Newfoundland in 1842

I REMEMBER the first Christmas Day I passed in Canada – being laughed at because I wandered out on to the plains near Peterboro', and brought in a wreath of the boxleaved trailing wintergreen (which with its scarlet berries reminded me of the varnished holly with which we were wont to garnish the old house at home), and hanging it over the mantel piece, and above the pictures of my host's parlor, in honor of the day. It seemed to me these green branches might be held as emblems to remind us that we should keep faith bright and green within our hearts.
   Catharine Parr Traill / Canadian Settler's Guide 1854

BIOGRAPHIES

Included here is brief biographical and bibliographical information on the people quoted or simply mentioned in the text. In square brackets after each biography the source of the information is indicated (short titles and abbreviations refer the reader to the general Bibliography on page 163). The works listed at the end of the entry are the sources of the quotations, with the appropriate page references indicated. Generally, we have given complete data for the version from which we quote and have indicated as well, where possible, the first publication and modern reprints and new editions.

Albanel, Charles 1616 (or 1613)–96
He was born in Auvergne and joined the Jesuit mission in Quebec in 1649. For many years he spent the winter at Tadoussac among the Montagnais, returning to Quebec in the spring or summer. Often considered as much an explorer as a missionary, he made many expeditions into the wilderness, including an overland expedition with Paul Denys de St Simon to Hudson Bay in 1671–2, the first Frenchmen to make the journey officially. On a second voyage to Hudson Bay in 1674, he was captured by the English and sent to Europe. Back in Canada in 1676, he laboured in the missions until his death at Sault Ste Marie.   [DCB I]
> *The Jesuit Relations* LVI (1671–72)
> rose: 207

Allouez, Claude Jean 1622–89
He came to Canada in 1658 as a Jesuit missionary and served at Trois-Rivières and other settlements along the St Lawrence. After 1665 he ministered in the west, among the Ottawas on Lake Superior and finally in the Illinois missions in what are now the states of Wisconsin, Michigan, and Minnesota. His territory included 3,000 miles of wild country inhabited by

23 Indian nations. He is reputed to have baptized some 10,000 neophytes. He wrote the earliest published account of the Illinois Indians and was a man of unique spiritual and linguistic gifts. He is particularly revered in Wisconsin, where a monument was erected to him at De Pere in 1899.   [DCB I]
> *Father Allouez's Journey To Lake Superior, 1665–1667* from *Early Narratives Of The Northwest 1634–1699* edited by Louise Phelps Kellogg. New York 1917. First published as a 'Jesuit Relation,' Paris 1688
> tripe de roche: 101

Anburey, Thomas dates unknown
Almost no biographical details are known until he sailed from Cork in the summer of 1776 in charge of Irish recruits of the 47th Regiment. He arrived in Quebec in October and served under General John Burgoyne at the disastrous battle of Saratoga. He was a prisoner in the United States until repatriated to Britain in 1781. He stayed in the army for one more year, then vanished into private life once more. His *Travels* was published in London in 1789 and has been a subject of controversy and entertainment ever since. It now seems clear that Anburey plagiarized extensively from Kalm,

Carver, and Burgoyne among others, but his compilation is written with such spirit and insight that it has been called 'the idealized memoir of each and every member of the Convention Army.' [*With Burgoyne from Quebec* ed Sidney Jackman, Toronto 1963]

Travels Through The Interior Parts of America, 1771–1781 Boston and New York, 1923. 2 volumes. First published England 1789.
fir: 122-31; plantain: 2301; pine: 24, 521; spruce: 81-21; walnut: 52-31

Avaugour, Louis d' 1669–1732

He joined the Jesuits in Paris at the unusually advanced entrance age of 27. He completed his novitiate but came to Quebec before receiving holy orders. He was given minor orders by Bishop Saint-Vallier in the chapel of the Quebec seminary in 1699. His first mission was served at Lorette where he quickly acquired a deep understanding of the character of the Hurons. In 1710 he sent a long report on the state of the mission to the Jesuit superior in Canada, wherein he warned that drunkenness would not only lead the Indians to reject Christianity, but would eventually cause France to lose the colony. About 1720 Avaugour was sent to the Illinois mission where he remained until he was recalled to Paris in 1726 to become procurator for the Jesuits in both Canada and Louisiana. [DCB II]

Jesuit Relations LXVI (1702–12)
maidenhair: 155

Baffin, William 1584?–1622

Little is known of this brilliant navigator's life until his final ten years. He was probably a Londoner, self-educated and of humble origin but extraordinary ability. He was employed as a pilot by the Muscovy Company and the Northwest Company. He made several voyages to the Arctic during which he kept detailed and accurate astronomical and geographical observations. He mapped Lancaster Sound, the entrance to the Northwest Passage (although he did not realize this), and was also the first to figure a longitude at sea while under way. He later joined the East India Company and was killed at a siege of the Portuguese at Ormuz. Baffin Island is named after him. [DCB I]

The Voyages of William Baffin, 1612–1622 edited by Clements R. Markham. Published for the Hakluyt Society, London 1881
scurvy grass: 148

Beavan, Emily (Shaw) fl 1838–48

She is believed to have been born in Ireland, the daughter of a sea-captain who made many voyages to Saint John, New Brunswick. By the 1840s she was married to a physician who practised in New Brunswick. The couple returned to Ireland in 1848. She contributed romantic stories to the short-lived New Brunswick journal *Amaranth* and was the author of *Life in the Backwoods of New Brunswick.* [DCB file]

Life in the Backwoods of New Brunswick. London 1845
mayflower: 17

Biard, Pierre 1567 (or 1568)–1622

He was born at Grenoble and later studied and taught theology in France. In 1611 he was sent to Port-Royal in Acadia as a missionary where he incurred the enmity of the Biencourt family, commanders of the settlement. In 1613 with his companion Père Énemond Massé, he helped to found Saint-Sauveur. He was taken to Virginia as a prisoner by the English and returned to France but only after several harrowing experiences, which included storms at sea and a narrow escape from being hanged. He spent the remainder of his life in disputations with the Calvinists and as a military chaplain. His writings about the Indians are considered of great value. [DCB I]

Jesuit Relations II (1612–14), III (1611–16)
groundnut: 298 II, 259 III

Bishop, Charles 1765?–1810?

He entered the navy as a boy, became a midshipman, and served for ten years. In 1792 he joined the merchant navy, trading on the west coast of Africa. In September 1794, as captain of the *Ruby*, he sailed for the northwest coast of North America to collect furs for the Canton trade. He reached the Columbia River the following May. His subsequent life was fraught with difficulties. He eventually settled in New South Wales, Australia, where he became a significant figure. In 1804 he began to suffer from severe mental problems. By 1805 he was confined as a lunatic and sent home to England, a tragic end for a man who had traded in Africa, America, Australia, and Oceania. His journals and letters are important in Pacific literature. [DCB file]

The Journal and Letters of Captain Charles Bishop on the north-west coast of America, in the Pacific and in New South Wales, 1794–1799 edited by Michael Roe. Published

for the Hakluyt Society, Cambridge 1967
   wappatoo: 123

Bompas, William Carpenter 1834–1906
He was born in London, England, and after
ordination in 1865 came to North America as a
missionary to the Mackenzie River district. He
was, successively, the first bishop of
Athabaska, Mackenzie River, and Selkirk. He
died at Cariboo Crossing in the Yukon. His
History of the diocese of Mackenzie River describes the flora and fauna of the region and the
customs of the Indians as well as the work of the
Church of England there. He wrote several
other books, including primers in the Beaver
and Cree dialects.　[MAC, OX]
  History of the Diocese of Mackenzie River
  London 1888
    tobacco: 46-7

Bonnycastle, Sir Richard Henry 1791–1847
He served during the war of 1812 as a commissioned officer in the Royal Engineers and was
later their commandant, first in Upper Canada
and then in Newfoundland. He was knighted
for his services in the 1837–8 rebellion. He
travelled extensively through the colonies
when on leave and wrote four books describing
his experiences and observations.　[MAC]
  The Canadas in 1841 2 volumes. London
  1841
    fir: 5, 7, II; pine: 6–7 II
  *Newfoundland in 1842: A Sequel to 'The
  Canadas in 1841'* 2 volumes. London 1842
    clover: 312 I; dwarf dandelion: 314 I;
    hawthorn: 307 I; pitcher plant: 312 I;
    spruce: 292–3 I; wintergreen: 304 I

Brébeuf, Jean de 1593–1649
His ancestors are said to have been companions-
in-arms of William the Conqueror and of St
Louis, king of France. He was born in Normandy and came to Canada as a missionary in
1625. He spent several nomadic months with a
group of Montagnais Indians and then was sent
to work among the Hurons where he remained
until 1629. He then returned to France for several years before being sent back to Huronia in
1633 to become superior of the new mission.
After seven tumultuous years he returned to
Quebec. In 1644 he was sent once more to
Huronia and in March 1649 he was martyred at
Saint Ignace during the Iroquois raids. He was
canonized in 1930 and in 1940 Pius XII pro-
claimed him patron saint of Canada along with
his seven fellow martyrs. Brébeuf's surviving
writings include two of the *Relations*. His
account of the Hurons is an invaluable record of
their doomed civilization.　[DCB I]
  Jesuit Relations VIII (1634–6)
    cedar: 105

Brooke, Frances (Moore) 1724?–89
An Englishwoman who conducted a weekly
periodical in 1755 entitled *The Old Maid*, she
married c 1756 the Reverend John Brooke who
became garrison chaplain at Quebec. After
joining him there in 1763, she wrote the first
Canadian novel which was published in England in 1769. *The History of Emily Montague*
is a lively epistolary romance, filled with col-
ourful details of Quebec life including 'much
hospitality ... scandal, dancing and good chear.'
She returned to England in 1768 where she was
a respected literary figure – friend of Samuel
Richardson, acquaintance of Fanny Burney,
and also the successful author of novels, a
tragedy, and two comic operas.　[DCB IV]
  The History of Emily Montague Introduction by Carl F. Klinck. Toronto 1961. First
  published London 1769
    strawberry: 192

Cartier, Jacques 1491?–1557
He was born in St Malo, Brittany. Nothing is
known about his career before 1532. In 1534 he
was commissioned by François I to make a voy-
age of exploration in the gulf of the St Law-
rence. After passing through the Strait of
Belle-Isle, he sailed along the coast of Labrador
which he described as 'the land that God gave to
Cain.' On this same journey he also discovered
Prince Edward Island and explored the Gaspé.
In 1535 he made a second voyage on the *Grande
Hermine*, this time with three ships and 110
men. He ascended the St Lawrence as far as
Hochelaga (now Montreal), spent the winter at
Stadacona, near the site of what is now Quebec
City and returned to France in 1536. He made a
third voyage in 1541, this time subordinate to
the Sieur de Roberval. His later years were
spent as a businessman on his estate of
Limoilou in Brittany.　[DCB I]
  *A Shorte and Brief Narration (Cartier's Sec-
  ond Voyage) 1535–1536*, from *Early English
  and French Voyages, chiefly from Hakluyt,
  1534–1608* edited by Henry S. Burrage. New
  York 1906. *Bref récit* first published in Paris
  1545
    cedar: 75-7

Champlain, Samuel de c1570–1635
Champlain is known as the Father of New
France. He was born in Brouage, France, but his
birth date is unknown because the parish records were destroyed. Little about his parentage
or early life is recorded and no authoritative
portrait exists. In 1603 he made his first voyage
to Canada, as a private passenger on a ship
commanded by Gravé Du Pont, visiting the
Gulf of St Lawrence. In 1604 he accompanied
de Monts as geographer to Acadia where he
spent the next three years exploring and map-
ping the coast, spending the winter of 1606–7 at
Port-Royal where he founded the famous
Order of Good Cheer. In 1608 he was in charge
of an expedition to Quebec, where he built a
habitation. In 1612 he became commandant in
New France; in 1627 he became governor although he never received an official commission. A distinguished explorer, geographer,
and colonizer, he seems also to have been a
kindly, jovial, patient, and moral man.
[DCB I]
  *The Voyages and Explorations of Samuel de
  Champlain, 1604–1616, Narrated by Himself translated by Annie Nettleson Bourne,
  together with 'The Voyage of 1603,' reprinted from 'Purchas His Pilgrimes'* edited
  by Edward Gaylord Bourne. 2 volumes. New
  York 1922. Reprinted New York 1973. First
  published Paris 1632.
    bloodroot: 13 II; blueberry: 62 II; cedar: 15
    II; may apple: 70 II; walnut: 188–9 II
  *Voyages of Samuel de Champlain
  1604–1608* edited by W.L. Grant in *Original
  Narratives of Early American History* New
  York 1907
    corn: 62

Charlevoix, Pierre-François-Xavier de 1682–
1761
He became a Jesuit novice in Paris in 1698 and
was sent to Canada in 1705, where he taught
grammar in the college in Quebec. In 1709 he
returned to Paris and continued his studies,
becoming a professor in the Collège Louis-le-
Grand. In 1720 he was commissioned by the
government to investigate a route to the western sea. He visited posts on the Great Lakes and
travelled down the Mississippi as far as New
Orleans, returning to France after an absence of
2½ years. He wrote a history of New France, a
valuable journal with botanical notes, a life of

Mère Marie de l'Incarnation, and histories of
Japan, Paraguay, and Saint-Domingue. [DCB
III]
  Journal Of A Voyage To North-America
  London 1761. 2 volumes. First published
  France 1744
    corn: 122–3 II; ginseng: 99 II; poison ivy:
    17 II; sunflower: 250 I

Cheadle, Walter Butler 1835–1910
He was born in Lancashire and educated as a
physician at Cambridge. In 1862, with Lord
Milton, he set out to explore the North West
Territories, visiting Fort Pitt, Kamloops, and
the Cariboo goldmines and Victoria. The joint
account of their trip, frequently attributed to
Milton, has been discovered to have been written by Cheadle. He returned to Britain and
enjoyed a distinguished career as a doctor.
[MAC; DNB]
  Journal Of Trip Across Canada 1862–1863
  introduction by A.G. Doughty and Gustave
  Lanctot. Ottawa 1931. Reprinted Edmonton
  1971
    fungus: 51

Cook, James 1728–79
England's great navigator was born in Yorkshire, the son of a labourer. He joined the Royal
Navy as an able seaman in 1755 and by 1757
had passed his master's exams. He served during the Seven Years' War at the sieges of Louis-
bourg and Quebec, and later spent five years
charting the coast of Newfoundland. In 1768 as
captain of the *Endeavour* he sailed to the Pacific
on the first of two voyages which revo-
lutionized European knowledge of geography.
He explored the coasts of New Zealand, the east
coast of Australia, and part of New Guinea. On
his final expedition, which left England in 1776,
he entered Nootka Sound and gradually
explored as far north as the Bering Strait. He
was killed in 1779 by natives on the Sandwich
Islands. [DCB IV]
  *The Voyage Of The 'Resolution' and 'Dis-
  covery' 1776–1780* edited by J.C. Beagle-
  hole. 2 volumes. Published for the Hakluyt
  Society, Cambridge 1967
    garlic: 310 I

Denys, Nicolas 1598–1688
He was born in Tours into 'a family of engineers.' Although he apparently received little
formal education, by 1632 he was a merchant

and agent of the Compagnie de la Nouvelle-France at La Rochelle with the responsibility of finding volunteers and supplies for an expedition to Acadia to take possession of the country and to establish a colony. So began Denys' lengthy connection with Acadia. He established a fishery at what is now Liverpool, Nova Scotia, the first in a series of lumbering, fishing, and fur-trading enterprises that ranged from Cape Breton to New Brunswick to the Gaspé. Misfortune and the enmity of French rivals plagued this man of vision (at one time he was chained and placed in a dungeon in Port-Royal) so that his strenuous efforts did not lead to the permanent great seigneury of his dreams. In 1653 he bought the rights to the coast and islands of the Gulf of St Lawrence from Cap Canso to Cap des Rosiers on the Gaspé from the Compagnie. Shortly thereafter he became governor and lieutenant-general of this enormous area. But he continued to be haunted by bad luck and he died in poverty, probably in New Brunswick. At the age of 70 he became an author. His two-volume history of Acadia, published in France in 1672, is regarded as a classic.   [DCB I]

> The Description and Natural History of the Coasts of North America translated and edited by William F. Ganong. The Champlain Society, Toronto 1908. First published France 1672
>
>   ash: 381; beech: 377; raspberry: 147

Dièreville, Sieur de fl 1699–1711
Even his first name is unknown, as are his birth and death dates. Before 1699, according to his own account, he studied surgery in Paris and before 1701 he published some poems in the *Mercure galant*. The most significant event in his life was his journey to Acadia in 1699. He reached Port-Royal in October and spent a year there observing the region and its French and Indian inhabitants and gathering plants. After his return to France he became a surgeon at Pont-l'Évêque, where he is last heard of in 1711. His fame rests on his *Relation* (Rouen 1708), half in prose and half in verse, which went through three printings in one year. Approximately 25 specimens of Acadian plants in the herbarium of the Musée de l'histoire naturelle in Paris are labelled with his name. The species *Diervilla* (honeysuckle) was named after him by Tournefort.   [DCB II]

> *Relation of the Voyage to Port Royal in Acadia or New France* translated by Mrs

Clarence Webster, edited by John Clarence Webster. The Champlain Society, Toronto 1933. First published France 1708
>   fir: 176; fungus: 107; maple: 117

Dollier de Casson, François 1636–1701
This soldier-priest was born in Lower Brittany and served in his youth as a cavalry officer under Maréchal de Turenne. He then entered a Sulpician seminary and in 1666 he came to Canada as a missionary. After varied activities, including a stint as a military chaplain, he was sent with La Salle and de Galinée to try to reach the Mississippi in 1669. After being abandoned by La Salle near what is now Hamilton, the two Sulpicians proceeded to the north shore of Lake Erie, where they wintered, living off the flora and fauna of the land. From 1671–4 and 1678–1701 Dollier was superior of the Sulpicians and thus seigneur of Montreal. He was a gifted administrator, diplomat, and the first historian of Montreal. The range of his activities is astounding. He laid out the first streets for the city in 1672. He also drew up the plans, chose the site, and had the parish church of Notre Dame built. He encouraged education and attempted for 20 years 'the great undertaking' of the digging of the Lachine Canal. His *Histoire du Montréal* was discovered in Paris in 1844. The Indians said of him: 'There is a man!'   [DCB II]

> See Galinée

Douglas, David 1798–1834
He was born in Scotland. After working in the Botanical Garden of Glasgow, where he attracted the attention of W.J. Hooker, he was appointed botanical collector in the United States for the Royal Horticultural Society in 1823. He visited Oregon and California in 1824 and reached Fort Vancouver in 1825. In 1827 he travelled thence to Hudson Bay, where he met Sir John Franklin, with whom he returned to England. In 1829 he revisited the west coast of America and then went to the Hawaiian Islands where, in 1834, he was gored to death by an enraged wild bull. He identified and described many new plants including the Douglas fir species.   [DNB; MAC]

> *Journal Kept by David Douglas During His Travels in North America 1823–27* London 1914
>   lupine: 61

Drummond, Thomas d 1835
Little is known of Drummond's early life in
Scotland except that he ran a nursery in Forfar
c 1814 and later contributed information for
Hooker's *Flora Scotica* (1821). As assistant
naturalist to John Richardson, he accompanied
Franklin's second Arctic expedition as far as
Cumberland House in Saskatchewan and was
then sent on an independent botanizing trip to
the Rockies. He went with the Hudson Bay
Brigade as far as the Rocky Mountain Portage
in mid-October. There he hired an Indian
hunter and set off. His guide left him in January
and did not return until March. Drummond
thus spent two months of his first Canadian
winter entirely alone, relying on what he could
shoot for food, in a particularly severe winter.
Between 1831 and 1835 he travelled and
botanized in the southern United States to New
Orleans and Texas. He died in Havana.   [DNB;
Plant Hunters]

Ellis, Henry 1721–1806
He went as hydrographer, surveyor, and
mineralogist on an expedition to Hudson Bay in
1746 and wrote an account of the journey. From
1758–60 he was governor of Georgia. He was
appointed governor of Nova Scotia in 1761 but
did not undertake his duties and was replaced in
1763. He was involved with the Royal Procla-
mation of 1763 that established civil government in Quebec.   [MAC; OX]
    *A Voyage to Hudson's-Bay, by the 'Dobbs
    Galley and California' in the Years 1746 and
    1747* London 1748
        labrador tea: 168–70; wintergreen:
        168–70

Ewing, Juliana Horatia (Gatty) 1841–85
She was born in Yorkshire, the daughter of the
redoubtable Mrs Gatty. She married Major
Alexander Ewing in 1867 and spent the next
two years stationed in Fredericton, New
Brunswick. She was the author of *Jackanapes*
and other popular children's books. Several of
her stories have Canadian settings. Much of her
work appeared in *Aunt Judy's Magazine* which
was started by her mother in 1866. It lasted for
twenty years and was an influential voice in
Victorian children's literature.   [MAC; DCB
file]
    *Leaves from Juliana Horatia Ewing's
    'Canada Home'* gathered by Elizabeth S.
    Tucker. Boston 1896
        trillium: 138

Fergusson, Adam 1783–1862
He was born in Perthshire, Scotland, and was a
wealthy lawyer, a well-known agriculturalist,
and Reformer. After a visit to Canada and the
United States in 1831 he published *Practical
Notes*; there was a second edition in 1834 after
another visit. He settled with his family in
Upper Canada, founded Fergus and introduced
purebred Shorthorns. He was appointed a
member of the Legislative Council of Upper
Canada in 1839 and then of the Legislative
Council of Canada. He also became president of
the Agricultural Association of Upper Canada
which he had helped form in 1846.   [DCB IX]
    *Practical Notes Made During A Tour in
    Canada And A Portion of the United States
    in 1831* 2nd edition Edinburgh 1834. First
    published Edinburgh 1831
        sassafras: 121

Fidler, Peter 1769–1822
He was born in Derbyshire and apprenticed to
the Hudson's Bay Company in 1788. He
studied surveying with Philip Turnor and also
became a meteorologist. He built five northern
fur-trading posts between 1791 and 1802. From
1796 to 1821 he was chief surveyor for the
company. After finishing his survey of the Red
River Colony in 1813, he established a fort
there in 1817–18. He also surveyed the district
of Assiniboia. He spent 34 years of his life in the
service of the company. His *Journal* was published by the Champlain Society in 1934 but
other journals remain unpublished in the archives of the Hudson's Bay Company in
Winnipeg.   [DCB file]
    *Journal of a Journey overland from Buck-
    ingham House to the Rocky Mountains in
    1792 & 3* Hudson's Bay Company Archives
    E.3/2
        cactus: f32

Fisher, Peter 1782–1848
He was New Brunswick's first historian. He
was born on Staten Island, New York, and
brought by his parents to Saint John in 1783
and later to St Ann's Point (now Fredericton).
He became a successful lumber merchant. His
Sketches of New Brunswick (1825) and *Notitiæ
of New Brunswick* (1838) were published
anonymously.   [MAC]
    Sketches of New Brunswick 1825
        fiddlehead: 128

Franklin, Sir John 1786–1847
He joined the Royal Navy in 1800 and fought

under Nelson at Trafalgar. In 1819 he was put in command of an expedition to explore the Arctic coast eastward from the mouth of the Coppermine River. He returned in 1822 after experiencing near-starvation and many other dangers. The story of the party's sufferings is one of the most terrible on human record. His *Narrative* was published in 1823. On a second expedition in 1825–7 he explored the Arctic coast from both the east and west sides of the mouth of the Mackenzie River, and a second *Narrative* describes this journey. From 1836 to 1843 he was lieutenant-governor of Van Diemen's Land. On his third and last voyage to the Arctic, begun in 1845, his two ships were trapped by ice and all aboard eventually perished. Nearly fifty expeditions were sent to search for Franklin's party between 1847 and 1857 when the mystery of his fate was finally solved by Captain McClintock.   [MAC; DNB]

Narrative Of A Journey To The Shores Of The Polar Sea In The Years 1819, 20, 21, And 22 Edmonton 1970. First published London 1823

labrador tea: 362–3; strawberry: 88

Frobisher, Sir Martin   1539?–94
In his youth he went on two trading expeditions to Guinea where he was once detained for several months as a hostage by an African chief. This swashbuckling mariner was one of Queen Elizabeth's cherished privateers. He served in Ireland and harried French and Spanish ships alike. An early advocate of the search for a north-west passage to China, he made his first Arctic voyage under the auspices of the Muscovy Company in 1576, as admiral and pilot, and discovered the strait (in reality a deep bay) that he named after himself. He also discovered a black ore which supposedly contained gold. Consequently, he was sent on two more expeditions to mine for the precious metal, but they were failures. In 1585 as a vice-admiral under Sir Francis Drake he did strike gold – on a privateering expedition to the West Indies which took £60,000 of booty. He was knighted for his distinguished services against the Spanish Armada. He died at Plymouth from a wound received while storming a fort held by the Spanish.   [DCB I]

First Voyage, 1576 from *Voyages of the Elizabethan Seamen to America* edited by Edward John Payne. Second edition Oxford 1893.
94

Galinée, René de Bréhant de   c 1645–78
He was born in the diocese of Rennes of an ancient family whose motto was 'The pledged word of a Bréhant is better than silver.' He came to Canada as a Sulpician in 1668 after training in astronomy, mathematics, and theology. In 1669 he accompanied Dollier and La Salle on their Mississippi expedition. He later drew a map of the Great Lakes and wrote an interesting account of their voyage. Dollier destroyed his own manuscript because he considered Galinée's to be superior. He returned to France in 1671.   [DCB I]

The Journey of Dollier and Galinée by Galinée, 1669–70. From *Early Narratives Of The Northwest 1634-1699* edited by Louise Phelps Kellogg, New York 1917. First published by the Historical Society of Montreal 1875

grape: 196; sunflower: 182

Gaultier, Jean-François   1708–56
He was appointed king's physician in 1741 as successor to Michel Sarrazin, but did not come to Canada until 1742. He was also physician of Hôtel-Dieu and the Quebec Seminary. In 1745 he was elected a corresponding member of the Académie royale des sciences. In 1747, at the request of the governor, the Marquis de la Galissonière, he wrote a memoir to the commandants of all the forts in New France asking their assistance in collecting and cataloguing specimens, which Gaultier then sent on to Paris. When Peter Kalm visited Canada in 1749, Gaultier acted as his guide on botanical excursions around Quebec. In appreciation, the Swedish naturalist dedicated the genus *Gaultheria* (wintergreen) to him. He appears as a likable minor character in William Kirby's *The Golden Dog.*

Like Sarrazin, he was a man of diverse talents: physician, meteorologist, astronomer, mineralogist, and above all botanist. In November 1742 he set up the first meteorological station in Canada. Between 1742 and 1756 he kept a daily log which remained unknown for two centuries. A four-hundred-page manuscript on the plants of Canada was not discovered until 1951.   [DCB III (appendix)]

Goldie, John   1793–1886
He was born in Ayrshire and studied under Sir William Hooker at Glasgow's Botanic Gardens. He visited North America from 1817 to 1819 but was pursued by astonishingly bad luck: his

specimens were either lost or shipwrecked three times and he had little to show for his efforts. He later worked in Russia and Siberia. He emigrated to Canada in 1844 and settled with his family near Ayr, Upper Canada. He identified and described a fern *Aspidium goldianum* which was later named after him. [MAC; Goldie *Diary*]

> *Diary Of A Journey Through Upper Canada and Some of the New England States, 1819* Toronto 1967. Original ms in the Metropolitan Toronto Public Library
> hawthorn: 21

Gosse, Philip Henry 1810–88
He was born at Worcester, England. In 1827 he became clerk in a whaler's office at Carbonear, Newfoundland. He relieved the boredom of his job through his studies as a naturalist. For a time he farmed unsuccessfully in Lower Canada. After travels in the United States he returned to England in 1839. His *Canadian Naturalist*, written on the voyage and published in 1840, launched his career as the author of many popular books on zoology, illustrated with his own meticulous drawings. An ardent member of the Plymouth Brethren, he was an opponent of the theory of evolution. Sir Edmund Gosse described their unusual family relationship in *Father and Son*. [DNB; OX]

> *The Canadian Naturalist, 1840: A Series of Conversations on the Natural History of Lower Canada* London 1840. Reprinted Toronto 1971
> balm: 163; dandelion: 162

Graham, Andrew d 1815
This long-forgotten naturalist was the victim of an incredibly involved case of plagiarism and only recently has his book *Observations on Hudson's Bay* been published in its entirety. He was a Scot who emigrated to Churchill, Manitoba, in 1749 as servant to the sloopmaster. In 1753 he went to York Factory as clerk and accountant under James Isham. He spent the following years in various posts until in 1774 he became chief at Prince of Wales's Fort at Churchill. In 1775 he retired to Edinburgh. In 1771–2 he wrote the decisive memorandum which led to the founding of Cumberland House by Samuel Hearne and the true beginning of the battle with the Nor'Westers. [*Observations*]

> *Observations on Hudson's Bay 1767–1791* edited by Glyndwr Williams. London 1969.

Hudson's Bay Records Society, volume 27
> bedstraw: 135

Hardy, Campbell 1831–1919
He was an officer in the Royal Artillery and served in the Maritimes for 15 years, chiefly in Halifax. He was a keen sportsman-naturalist and artist who wrote articles on sports and two books on hunting. His *Forest Life in Acadie* (1869) combines information about the flora and fauna of the provinces with memories of sports, camping, and caribou hunting in Newfoundland, and watercolour sketches. He was one of the founders of the Nova Scotia Institute of Natural History. [MAC; OX; DCB file]

> *Forest Life in Acadie* London 1869
> aster: 111; cranberry: 200; groundnut: 1, 168; hemlock: 31–2; mayflower: 309–10

Harmon, Daniel Williams 1778–1843
He was born in Vermont and joined the Nor'Westers in 1800. He spent nineteen years in the North West and kept a detailed journal that recounts the daily activities, thoughts, and journeys of a fur-trader. In 1805 he married a Métis woman by whom he had fourteen children. His journals were extensively edited by the Reverend Daniel Haskel and were published in Andover in 1820. [MAC; OX; DCB file]

> *Sixteen Years In The Indian Country* edited by W. Kaye Lambe. Toronto 1957
> rose: 72
> *A Journal Of Voyages And Travels In The Interior Of North America* Andover 1820
> nettle: 291

Head, Sir George 1782–1855
The brother of Sir Francis Bond Head, governor of Upper Canada during the 1837 rebellion, he was educated at Charterhouse. In 1809 he became a clerk in the commissariat department of the British army and served in the Peninsular War. He was promoted and sent to Canada in 1814 and was stationed at Halifax, Quebec, and on Lake Huron. In 1823 he was placed on half-pay. He was a deputy knight marshal at the coronations of both William IV and Queen Victoria. Among his works are a translation of Apuleius and *Forest scenes and incidents*, his Canadian reminiscences. [MAC; DNB]

> *Forest Scenes And Incidents in the Wilds of North America* 2nd edition London 1838. First published London 1829
> basswood: 190–1; birch: 283; leeks: 241

Hearne, Samuel 1745–92
He was born in London, England, the son of a

prominent engineer who died when Hearne was three. He joined the Royal Navy at eleven and served during the Seven Years' War. In 1766 he joined the Hudson's Bay Company and was sent to Fort Prince of Wales. He made three journeys of exploration between 1769 and 1772; on the third he reached the Arctic Ocean at the mouth of the Coppermine River, thus becoming the first European to reach the Arctic Ocean overland. He was also the first European to see and cross Great Slave Lake. He built Cumberland House, the first western inland post, in 1774 and was appointed governor of Fort Prince of Wales in 1775. After its capture by the French under Comte de Lapérouse in 1782, he was allowed to go back to England. He returned to Churchill in 1783 and rebuilt the fort on a new site. He retired to England in 1787 and spent the rest of his life preparing his *Journey from Prince of Wales's Fort* for publication. It appeared posthumously.   [DCB IV]
> *A Journey From Prince of Wales's Fort in Hudson's Bay To The Northern Ocean. In the Years 1769, 1770, 1771 & 1772* Edmonton 1971. First published London 1795
>> cranberry: 449; dandelion: 457; tripe de roche: 328

Hébert, Louis   1575?–1627
Canada's first colonist was an apothecary. Even when he accompanied de Monts' expedition to Acadia he attempted agriculture at Port-Royal. After several visits to the New World, in 1617 he was persuaded by Champlain to settle with his family in Quebec where he commenced farming. At the time of his death (as the result of a fall on the ice) he had grain fields, vegetable gardens, and an apple-orchard planted with trees from Normandy, all achieved using only handtools.   [DCB I]

Henry, Alexander   1739–1824
He was born in New Jersey. He was one of the first English traders to come to Michilimackinac after the British conquest of Canada and was almost murdered there in 1763 during Pontiac's Conspiracy. He was one of the pioneers in the Canadian fur-trade, for some years trading on Lake Superior and later at posts along the Saskatchewan River. By 1781 he had settled in Montreal as a merchant. He sold out his fur-trading interests to the North West Company but remained a silent partner until 1796. His *Travels and Adventures in Canada* is a classic

and was one of the main sources used by Francis Parkman for *The Conspiracy of Pontiac*.   [MAC; OX]
> *Travels And Adventures In Canada and the Indian Territories Between the Years 1760 and 1776* edited by James Bain. New York 1969. First published Boston 1901

Henry, Alexander, the younger   d 1814
He was the nephew of Alexander Henry. He joined the North West Company as a clerk c 1792 and spent the next twenty-two years travelling in the North West and to the Pacific. He became a partner of the company between 1799 and 1802. He was drowned off Fort George on the Pacific coast, 22 May 1814. His diaries and notebooks, edited by Elliott Coues, together with the journals of David Thompson, were published in 1897.   [MAC]
> *The Manuscript Journals of Alexander Henry … And David Thompson, 1799–1814* from *New Light On The Early History Of The Greater Northwest* edited by Elliott Coues. 3 volumes. New York 1897
>> bittersweet: 172 I

Heriot, George   1759–1839
He was educated in Edinburgh and the Royal Military Academy at Woolwich, where he studied art under Paul Sandby. In 1792 he went to Quebec as clerk in the Ordnance Department. From 1799 to 1816 he was deputy postmaster general of British North America, even then a controversial post. He travelled extensively during these years, always continuing his second career as a watercolourist. He wrote a *History of Canada* and *Travels through the Canadas*, the latter embellished by his own enchanting paintings.   [MAC; *George Heriot Painter of the Canadas* Gerald Finley. Agnes Etherington Art Centre, Kingston 1978]
> *Travels Through the Canadas* London 1807. Reprinted Toronto 1971
>> birch: 283; cedar: 165; corn: 311; ginseng: 226

Hood, Lieutenant Robert   1796–1821
This young Royal Navy topographer accompanied Franklin's 1819 expedition to the Arctic. He kept a journal which was incorporated in the *Narrative* and did watercolour drawings of birds and other subjects. He was murdered by his Indian guide in the Barrens.   [*Franklin: Narrative* 175–6; Harper]

Howison, John dates unknown
He spent two and a half years in Upper Canada
(1818–20). His *Sketches of Upper Canada*
(Edinburgh 1821) is one of the best of the travel
books of the period, describing the advantages
and disadvantages of emigration to the New
World. Howison thought the province a good
place for poor farmers but emphasized that the
state of its civilization was low. He deplored
'the high pretensions ... assuming style of
manners, and ... vain display of general knowledge' compared with the 'placid contentment'
of the more docile English peasant. He published several other travel books including a
two-volume work *European Colonies in Various Parts of the World*. [OX; Craig]
   Sketches of Upper Canada Edinburgh 1821
     hickory: 118

Isham, James 1716?–61
He was born in London and joined the Hudson's
Bay Company as a 'writer' in 1732, being in-
structed in book-keeping at York Fort (York
Factory). He served them continuously thereafter until his death there. His writings are
considered a basic source for studies on the
eighteenth-century fur trade – in particular the
difficulties and challenges facing the company –
and for the flora and fauna of the far north. His
ideas inspired that other pioneer naturalist Andrew Graham. He was revered by the traders
and was 'the Idol of the Indians.' [DCB III]
   Isham's Observations and Notes 1743–1749
   edited with an introduction by E.E. Rich. The
   Champlain Society, Hudson's Bay Series,
   volume 12. Toronto 1949
     217; 132n

James, Captain Thomas 1593?–1635?
He was born in Bristol and became a barrister,
but then turned to the sea. In 1631 he was
commissioned by the Bristol Society of Merchant Venturers to search for a northwest passage to Asia. His expedition to Hudson Bay
underwent a series of tribulations. He explored
James Bay, which is named after him, and
wintered off Charlton Island, the first inten-
tional wintering of a European party in the
North. James' conviction that no passage
existed south of 66' N discouraged further exploration in the region for many years. His
account of his expedition is considered a classic.
Some critics think that Coleridge drew on it
when writing *The Rime of the Ancient Mariner*

and Robert Boyle quoted it extensively in his
treatise on the subject of cold. [DCB I]
   *The Strange and Dangerous Voyage of
   Captain Thomas James* edited by W.A.
   Kenyon. Toronto 1975. First published by
   the Hakluyt Society, London 1894
     vetch: 101

Jameson, Anna Brownell (Murphy)
1794–1860
She was born in Dublin, the daughter of a
talented miniaturist. In 1825 she married
Robert Sympson Jameson, a barrister, who was
to be appointed attorney general of Upper
Canada in 1833. The marriage was unsuccessful
and the couple soon separated, but she came to
Canada at his request in 1836. She left her
husband and the country in 1837 and returned
to an active literary life in London. She was an
industrious and skilful writer who published
books on women, travel, and art. Her *Winter
Studies and Summer Rambles*, published in
England in 1838, is still enjoyed for its fresh-
ness and accurate depiction of the life of Upper
Canada on the eve of the 1837 Rebellion.
[Jameson *Selections*]
   *Winter Studies and Summer Rambles in
   Canada: Selections* introduction by Clara
   Thomas. Toronto 1965. First published Lon-
   don 1838
     columbine: 159; water-lily: 157

Jewitt, John 1783–1821
He was an armourer on the American trading
ship the *Boston* which anchored at Nootka
Sound, Vancouver Island, in 1803. The crew
was soon massacred except for Jewitt and
one other. Jewitt was a slave of Maquinna, chief
of the Nootka Indians, until July 1805 when he
was released by Captain Hill of the *Lydia*. He
kept a journal of his experiences which has been
published many times. He died at Hartford,
Connecticut. [MAC; OX]
   *Narrative of the Adventures and Sufferings
   of John R. Jewitt, Only Survivor of the crew
   of the ship Boston, 1869* Washington 1967.
   First published Boston 1807
     blackberry: 45–6; strawberry: 44

Jolliet, Louis 1645?–1700
This man of many talents was born in Quebec
and educated at the Jesuit College there. He
abandoned minor orders to become a fur-

trader. In 1673 he and Marquette were sent by Frontenac and Talon to discover into which sea the Mississippi River flowed. The intrepid pair succeeded in reaching the boundaries of what is now Louisiana. They decided to turn back because of Native hostility and the risk of confrontation with the Spanish, but they had learned that the Mississippi flows into the Gulf of Mexico. Unfortunately the papers containing Jolliet's log and map were lost when his canoe capsized on the way back to Quebec and copies which he had left at Sault Ste-Marie were destroyed by fire. Jolliet became a merchant and, in 1679, travelled to Hudson Bay in connection with the fur-trade. A year later he was given the island of Anticosti where he hoped to set up fishing-grounds for cod, seals, and whales. After exploring and charting the coast of Labrador in 1694, he was appointed king's hydrographer. He also taught at the Jesuit College and was the first organist of the cathedral at Quebec.   [DCB I]

> The Mississippi Voyage of Jolliet and Marquette, 1673 from Early Narratives Of The Northwest 1634–1699 edited by Louise Phelps Kellogg. New York 1917
> rice: 230–1

Kalm, Peter (Pehr) 1716–79

A pupil and friend of Carl von Linné (Linneus), he was sent to North America in 1748 by the Swedish Academy of Sciences to study the flora and to collect specimens. He remained until 1751, travelling throughout Pennsylvania, New York, New Jersey, and southern Canada and making friends with such notables as Benjamin Franklin. After his return to Sweden (bringing with him a large collection of plants, seeds, insects, etc) he continued as professor of botany at the university of Åbo. In 1757 he was also ordained as a Lutheran minister. He was the first person to describe Niagara Falls in English from original observation. The manuscript of Kalm's Flora of Canada was probably destroyed in a fire at Åbo. Linnaeus named the American mountain laurel (Kalmia latifolia) after him.   [DCB IV; MAC]

> The America of 1750: Peter Kalm's Travels in North America edited by A.B. Benson. 2 volumes. New York 1927. Reprinted 1966. First published as Travels into North America. 3 volumes. London 1770–1
> basswood: 564; beech: 530; evening primrose: 538; grape: 481; reindeer moss: 447

Kane, Paul 1810–71

He was born in Ireland and brought to Canada as a young boy. After early painting lessons from an art teacher, he worked as a signpainter and then as a decorative painter in furniture factories in York and Cobourg. He spent five years in the United States painting portraits, then in 1841 sailed from New Orleans to Europe where he travelled and studied art. He met the American artist George Catlin in London and was convinced by his arguments of the importance of recording the Indians' customs and appearance. He returned to Toronto and spent the next four years (1845–8) travelling thousands of miles, recording more than 700 sketches. He spent the remainder of his life in Toronto painting canvases based on this work. Kane also kept a diary which was published in London in 1859 as Wanderings of an Artist. [DCB X]

> Wanderings Of An Artist London 1859
> camass: 186, 208; clover: 209; oak: 187 wappatoo: 186

Kelsey, Henry c 1667–1724

He was apprenticed to the Hudson's Bay Company in 1684. He served it in many significant ways for nearly forty years and eventually was appointed governor over all the bay settlements, including Churchill. However, his reputation rests chiefly on his great voyage of exploration from Hudson Bay to the plains of Saskatchewan in 1690–2. He is credited with being the first white man in the Canadian west to describe the grizzly bear and the buffalo, which he portrayed in crude but endearing verse in his journal. Historians did not know of The Kelsey Papers until 1926. [DCB II]

> The Kelsey Papers edited by Arthur G. Doughty and Chester Martin. Ottawa 1929
> chokecherry: 3

Lafitau, Joseph-François c 1681–1746

He was born in Bordeaux, the son of a wine merchant and banker. After a thorough Jesuit education he came to Quebec as a missionary. He served at Sault-Saint-Louis (Caughnawaga) from 1712 to 1717. His Mémoire to the Duc d'Orléans (1718) written after his return to France, describing how he found ginseng in Canada, made him famous in Europe. He also wrote, among other works, a highly regarded two-volume study of the customs of Native peoples. He has been praised for taking 'the first step towards ethnological research for its own sake.' [DCB III]

Lahontan, Louis-Armand de Lom d'Arce, Baron de 1666–1715?
He apparently came to Canada in 1683 as a young officer. After various military activities and travels this favourite of Frontenac was made king's lieutenant in Placentia, Newfoundland. After many disagreements with the governor, he was accused of insubordination and forced to flee in 1693. He spent the rest of his life wandering through Europe in exile and writing his memoirs which were published in The Hague in 1703. A lively if often unreliable account of his experiences in Canada, of Indian customs, and of flora and fauna, they have gone through many editions and translations.
[DCB II]
New Voyages to North-America. Reprinted from the English edition of 1703 edited by Reuben Gold Thwaites. 2 volumes. Chicago 1905. First published The Hague 1703
blueberry: 372 I; cherry: 367 I; maidenhair: 372 I; maple: 366–7 I; oak: 325–6 I

Lalemant, Jérôme 1593–1673
He entered the Jesuit novitiate in Paris in 1610. After many years in education, he came to Canada in 1638 and was at once made Jean de Brébeuf's successor as superior of the Huron mission. He instituted the system of *donnés* ('given men') who dedicated their lives to the mission without taking religious vows. In 1644 he was appointed superior of the Jesuits in Canada but was later recalled to France. He returned to Quebec in 1659, again as superior. He was spiritual adviser to Marie de l'Incarnation, who called him the most saintly man she had known in her life. He wrote the *Relations* concerning the Hurons for the years 1639 to 1644 and several others. He also contributed to the invaluable *Journal des Jésuites*, a detailed record of the daily life of the colony. [DCB I]
Jesuit Relations XXXI (1647)
purslane: 91

Lambert, John c 1775–1816?
He was sent to Canada to encourage the growing of hemp when Napoleon threatened to cut off supplies from northern Europe. He arrived in 1806 and visited an uncle in Quebec. After a year there, during which time the project collapsed, Lambert spent six months in the United States. He returned to England in 1809 and wrote his impressions of the New World, including a very full account of French Canada. His three-volume *Travels*, published in 1810 with aquatints from his own drawings, quickly went through three editions. There is little further information about him except that he was a school-fellow of Colonel By. In 1811 he edited Washington Irving's essays for English publication. [DNB; Craig; Harper]
Travels Through Canada, and the United States of North America, In The Years 1806, 1807 & 1808 2 volumes. London 1814. First published London 1810 as *Travels Through Lower Canada*
milkweed: 437 I

Langton, John 1808–94
He was born in Lancashire and graduated from Trinity College, Cambridge, in 1829. After some uncertain years in Liverpool, he emigrated to Canada in 1833 and was followed in 1837 by his parents, aunt, and sister. He settled at Sturgeon Lake, near Fenelon Falls. After some years of farming and milling, he moved to Peterborough and became warden of the county. He was in the legislature from 1851–5. In 1855 he became auditor of public accounts and a year later vice-chancellor of the University of Toronto. After Confederation he became auditor general of the Dominion. His letters, edited by his son, were published in 1926. Like the journals of his sister Anne (edited by H.H. Langton and published in 1960 as *A Gentlewoman in Upper Canada*) they are a valuable record of pioneer life. [Langton *Early Days*]
Early Days In Upper Canada, Letters of John Langton ... 1833–37 edited by W.A. Langton. Toronto 1926
nettle: 30

La Rochefoucauld-Liancourt, François Alexandre Frédéric, Duc de 1747–1827
Although an aristocrat, the son of the Duc d'Estissac, master of the robes to the king of France, he was elected to the States-General in 1789 and became president of the Assemblée nationale. During the Terror he was forced to flee to England. He spent 1795–7 travelling in North America. He returned to France in 1799 to an active literary – although not political – career. His *Voyage dans les Etats-Unis d'Amérique*, published in Paris in 8 volumes in 1799, contains an interesting account of his stay in Upper Canada. [MAC]

Travels Through The United States of North America, The Country of the Iroquois, and Upper Canada, in the years 1795, 1796 and 1797; with an Authentic Account of Lower Canada 2 volumes. London 1799. First published France 1799

rice: 292 I; sassafras: 261 I

Le Clercq, Chrestien 1641 – still living in 1700

He was a Recollet who came to Quebec in 1675 and travelled as an itinerant missionary from Gaspé to the Miramichi River. He invented a system of hieroglyphics that is still the basis of that used by the Micmac. Le Clercq returned to France seeking permission to open a house in Montreal and a hospice at Quebec. After he sailed again for Quebec in the summer of 1681, little is known of his activities. In 1686 he left his Micmacs for the last time. By 1700 he was superior of the Recollets in Saint-Omer. Le Clercq's *Nouvelle Relation de la Gaspésie* (he was the first to use the term) was published in Paris in 1691 and is a valuable account of that area. He also wrote a history of the church in New France, praising the work of the Recollets and criticizing the Jesuits. He is ranked among the great historiographers of the colony. [DCB I]

New Relations of Gaspesia. Translated and edited with a reprint of the original William F. Ganong. The Champlain Society, volume 5. Toronto 1910. First published France 1691

maple: 122; tobacco: 298

Le Jeune, Paul 1591–1664

He was born in the province of Champagne into a Calvinist family. He became a Catholic and entered the Jesuit novitiate in 1613. By 1631 he was in charge of the Jesuit residence at Dieppe; the following year he was sent to Quebec where he was superior-general of the mission in Canada until 1639. He remained until 1649, serving as a simple missionary at Quebec, Sillery, Tadoussac, Trois-Rivières, and Montreal. After his return to France he was made procurator of the mission in Canada. He is regarded as the true founder of the Jesuit mission. He was the first editor of the famed Jesuit *Relations*. He wrote the first eleven himself and contributed to many others. [DCB I]

Jesuit Relations V (1632–3), VIII (1634–6), IX (1636), XVI (1639), XLIII (1656–7)

blueberry: 191 XVI; lily: 103 V; nettle: 255 IX; plums: 17 VIII; sassafras: 259 XLIII

Le Mercier, François-Joseph 1604–90

After early training in Paris he arrived in New France in 1635. Three days later he set off by canoe for the Huron country. He served at Ihonatiria under Jean de Brébeuf and quickly gained mastery of the Huron tongue. He spent the years until the Iroquois destruction of the missions in training new missionaries and supervising the *donnés* and servants of the household at Sainte-Marie-des-Hurons. In 1650, he and Father Ragueneau led the remnants of the Huron nation to Quebec. In 1653 he was appointed rector of the Collège at Quebec and superior-general of the missions in New France. His later years were spent in the West Indies missions. He wrote several of the *Relations* during his years in Canada. [DCB I]

Jesuit Relations XIII (1637)

strawberry: 231

Lescarbot, Marc c 1570–1642

He was born at Vervins, France and was called to the Parlement of Paris as a lawyer in 1599. He wrote, translated, and mingled with men of letters. In 1606 he accompanied de Poutrincourt to Canada, spending the winter in Acadia. After his return to France in 1607, he began his massive *Histoire de la Nouvelle-France*. It was published in 1609, with two subsequent editions in 1611 and 1617, and a German and two English translations. He also wrote a small collection of poems, an appendix to the *Histoire*. *Les muses de la Nouvelle-France* includes his masque *Le Théâtre de Neptune*, performed at Port-Royal in November 1606. This first theatrical production in North America boasted a court of Tritons and Aboriginals reciting verse in French, Gascon, and Souriquois to an accompaniment of trumpets and cannon. Lescarbot has been called 'the French Hakluyt' and 'the best of the historians of New France.' [DCB I]

Nova Francia: A Description of Acadia 1606 translated by P. Erondelle, 1609; introduction by H.P. Biggar, London 1928. First published France 1609

grape: 107; milkweed: 296; sassafras: 297–8

Long, John fl 1768–91

He came to Quebec as a merchant's clerk in 1768 and became so skilled in Native languages that he was hired as an interpreter. After fighting in the Revolution, he became a fur-trader in the Lake Nipigon area. He spent some time in the Loyalist settlements on the Bay of

Quinte and returned permanently to England in 1788. After the publication of his entertaining *Voyages and Travels* in 1791, nothing further is known of him.   [MAC]

> *Voyages And Travels Of An Indian Interpreter And Trader* London 1791. Reprinted Toronto 1971
>> blueberry: 45–6; tobacco: 46

Mackenzie, Sir Alexander 1764–1820
He was born near Stornoway on the island of Lewis and emigrated with his family to New York in 1774. He was sent to school in Montreal and in 1779 he became a clerk in a firm which was later to be taken over by the North West Company. When this occurred in 1787, he became a partner. He voyaged from Fort Chipewyan on Lake Athabaska to the Arctic Ocean by the Slave River, Great Slave Lake, and an unexplored 'River of Disappointment' which now bears his name. His epochal journey to the Pacific Ocean was made in 1792–3. He severed his connection with the Nor'Westers in 1799 and went to England where his *Voyages* were published in 1801. He returned to Canada and after taking part in various mercantile activities was elected to the Legislative Assembly of Lower Canada where he served for several years. He returned to Scotland in 1808.   [MAC; OX; DNB]

> *Voyages From Montreal Through The Continent Of North America* Edmonton 1971. First published London 1801
>> hemlock: 326–7

Marie-Victorin, Frère (Conrad Kirouac) 1885–1944
He was born at Kingsey Falls, Quebec, and entered the Order of the Christian Brothers in 1901. He became one of Canada's most distinguished scientists. In 1920 he was appointed professor of Botany at the University of Montreal, where he founded the Botanical Institute and Botanical Gardens. He wrote many books, both botanical and folkloric, including the magisterial *Flore laurentienne*.   [MAC; OX]

Marquette, Jacques 1637–75
He was born at Laon in northern France and was sent to Canada as a Jesuit missionary in 1666. He spent a year at Trois-Rivières studying Montagnais and other Indian languages – he was eventually fluent in six – and then worked among the Ottawas and Hurons. In 1671 he founded Saint-Ignace at Michilimackinac. Be-

cause of his linguistic talents he was sent with Jolliet on the epic journey down the Mississippi. In 1674 he attempted to found a mission among the Kaskaskia Indians in the Illinois territory but was forced to give up the project because of ill-health. He died in the wilderness on his way back to Saint-Ignace. Although there is considerable controversy among historians about his career, his name has been given to a railroad, a university, cities, streets, and a river.   [DCB I]

> See Jolliet
>> rice: 230–1

Masson, Francis 1741–1805
He was born in Aberdeen, Scotland, and trained at the Royal Botanic Gardens in Kew. He was the first gardener-collector sent out by the Gardens and he collected successfully in the Canary Islands, the Azores, the West Indies, Spain, Portugal, and Tangiers. In 1798 Masson came to Canada and travelled widely. In 1799 he went with traders as far as Grande Portage on Lake Superior. Tragically, both his career and health foundered in Canada and he died in Montreal.   [DNB; DCB file]

Menzies, Archibald 1754–1842
He was born in Perthshire, Scotland. As a young man he worked as a gardener in the Edinburgh Botanic Gardens and also obtained training as a surgeon at the university. He then entered the navy as assistant-surgeon and served against the French for several years. He was a botanist with Colnett on the fur-trading voyage of exploration in 1786 that sailed to America, the Sandwich Islands, and China. In 1790 he sailed as a naturalist and surgeon with Captain Vancouver on the *Discovery*. He collected plants and seeds both dried and living (kept in a glazed frame on the quarterdeck) and carried them back to Kew. His next posting was to the West Indies, after which he resigned and set up a practice in London. He became president of the Linnean Society.   [DNB; DCB file]

Moodie, Susanna (Strickland) 1803–85
She was born at Bungay, Suffolk, the daughter of Thomas Strickland of Reydon Hall. Agnes and Elizabeth Strickland, authors of *The Lives of the Queens of England* were sisters, as was Catharine Parr Traill. In 1831 she married Lieutenant J.W.D. Moodie of the 21st Fusiliers and in 1832 emigrated to Canada, settling first on a farm near Cobourg and later north of

Peterborough near her brother Samuel and sister. In 1839 she moved to Belleville where her husband had been appointed sheriff of Hastings County. She was, like the rest of her family, a prolific writer. Between 1839 and 1851 she contributed serials, sketches, and verses to the *Literary Garland*, a Montreal magazine. Her fame rests chiefly on that lively diatribe about life in Canada, *Roughing it in the bush*. Mrs Moodie's autocratic nature did not take kindly to the 'saucy familiarity' of servants and neighbours, but her attitudes were softened by time and she lived to write a heartfelt tribute to the land she came to appreciate. [MAC; OX]

Roughing It In The Bush or, Forest Life In Canada Toronto 1913. Reprinted Toronto 1962. First published 1852
  cardinal flower: 359; corn: 386; fungi: 479; harebell: 371; raspberry: 361; sumac: 323

Mountain, Bishop George Jehoshaphat 1789–1863
He was born in Norwich, England, the son of Jacob Mountain, the first Anglican bishop of Quebec. After graduating from Cambridge he returned to Quebec and became his father's secretary in 1811. He was ordained in 1814 and served in Fredericton, Quebec, and Montreal. In 1837 he was appointed bishop of Quebec. He administered the see until his death. An indefatigable traveller, he published sermons and journals and was the author of a book of poems *Songs of the Wilderness*. He was instrumental in founding both McGill and Bishop's universities. [DCB IX]

Visit To The Gaspé Coast 1824–1826 Québec 1943
  birch: 12
Songs Of The Wilderness ... 1844. Published for the benefit of Bishop's College at Lennoxville, London 1846
  lady's slipper: 22

Murray, Alexander Hunter 1818?–74
He was born in Scotland and served with the American Fur Company for several years before joining the Hudson's Bay Company as a senior clerk in the Mackenzie River District. In 1847 he was sent by the company to establish Fort Yukon in Russian Alaska. The company only relinquished the fort when the United States purchased Alaska. Later Murray became a chief trader and was put in charge of Lower Fort Garry. His *Journal of the Yukon* (1847–8),

illustrated by his own sketches, was published in 1910. [DCB X]
Journal of the Yukon 1847–48 edited by L.J. Burpee. Ottawa 1910
  tobacco: 43

Pond, Peter 1740–1807?
He was born in Connecticut and served as a soldier in the French and Indian wars. For ten years he was a fur-trader at Detroit and on the upper Mississippi. He made his first expedition to the North West in 1775. In 1778 he founded the first post in the Athabaska country and he may later have reached Great Slave Lake. In 1783 he became a partner in the North West Company but his implication in two murders caused his retirement from the fur trade in 1790. After his return to the United States, he was a special agent for the government in its dealings with Aboriginals. He died in New England, forgotten and poor. His maps of his expeditions to the North West were among the earliest drawn and hence of considerable significance. A fragment of his *Narrative* survived and has been published in several versions. [MAC]
The 'Narrative' of Peter Pond from *Five Fur Traders of the Northwest* edited by Charles M. Gates, introduction by Grace Lee Nute. Minneapolis 1933. First published in the *Connecticut Magazine* x, 2 (1906)
  rice: 33, 37

Pursh, Frederick 1774–1820
He was born in Saxony and worked at the Royal Botanic Gardens in Dresden. In 1799 he went to Baltimore. From 1802–5 he was in charge of the famous botanical garden of William Hamilton near Baltimore. He collected botanical specimens constantly and wrote the authoritative *Flora Americae Septentrionalis* (1814) the first complete flora of America north of Mexico. He later settled in Montreal and gathered materials (mainly in Quebec) for a flora of Canada. These were destroyed by fire and he died shortly afterwards, destitute. He is buried in Mount Royal Cemetery. [DAB]

Radisson, Pierre-Esprit c 1640–1710
Probably a native of Avignon, he came to Canada and was captured by the Iroquois sometime around 1651. On his second attempt, he escaped to Fort Orange (Albany, New York) in 1653. With his brother-in-law Chouart des Groseilliers, he made a voyage to the far end of

Lake Superior in 1659–60. His claims of reaching Hudson Bay are probably exaggerated, but he was probably the first white man to penetrate the North West. In 1665 the pair fell out with the French authorities and went to England where they witnessed the Great Plague and the Fire of London. Their willingness to lead a trading expedition to Hudson Bay eventually led to the foundation of the Hudson's Bay Company in 1670. After several years spent in switching allegiances, Radisson rejoined the Hudson's Bay Company permanently in 1684. He wrote a sometimes questionable but fascinating account of his journeys which contains much valuable material about Indian customs. It was discovered among Samuel Pepys' papers and first printed in 1885. [DCB II]

> *The Explorations of Pierre-Esprit Radisson from the original manuscript in the Bodleian Library and the British Museum* edited by Arthur T. Adams. Minneapolis 1961
> bittersweet: 132
> and from *Early Narratives Of The Northwest 1634–1699* edited by Louise Phelps Kellogg. New York 1917
> tripe de roche: 40–1

Ragueneau, Paul 1608–80
He was born in Paris and came to Canada as a missionary in 1636. A year later he was sent to the Huron country where he was subordinate to Brébeuf and Lalemant for eight years. He was superior in 1649 when the mission was attacked by the Iroquois and his was the heartbreaking decision to burn it. He escaped the martyrdom of his fellows and brought the 300 or so surviving Hurons to Quebec after first wintering with them on Christian Island in Georgian Bay. After returning to France in 1662, he succeeded Père Le Jeune as representative of the Jesuit missions in New France. He wrote the *Relations des Hurons* for 1646–50 which describe the doom of the mission. He also compiled memoirs of his martyred colleagues and wrote a life of Mère Catherine de Saint-Augustin, the mystic of Hôtel-Dieu at Quebec. [DCB I]

> *Jesuit Relations* XXXIV (1649)
> oak: 215, 225

Rale, Sébastien 1657–1724
He came to Canada as a Jesuit missionary in 1689 at the same time as Frontenac. His first mission was at the falls of the Chaudière River, where he learned Abenaki and began his

Abenaki-French dictionary. In 1691 he went to the Illinois mission at Kaskaskia. Two years later he was sent to Acadia, where, in 1694, he founded the mission to the Abenakis on the Kennebec River. He remained with his flock for thirty years as both a temporal and spiritual leader. During this period he incurred the enmity of the English who were contending for the region with the French and who placed a £100 reward on his head. On 23 August 1724 a group of New England militia attacked the mission and killed Rale. His dictionary, which had been carried off by soldiers, was published in 1833 with a memorial and notes by John Pickering. The manuscript is preserved at Harvard University. [DCB II]

> *Jesuit Relations* LXVII (1716–27)
> bayberry: 89

Richardson, Sir John 1787–1865
He was born in Dumfries, Scotland, the son of a wealthy brewer and friend of Burns. He studied medicine, botany, and geology at Edinburgh. He served in the Napoleonic wars as a naval surgeon from 1806 to 1814. He went with Sir John Franklin as surgeon-naturalist on two of his journeys to the Arctic; he was second in command of Franklin's second expedition and was in charge of the party that mapped the coast eastward from the Mackenzie to the Coppermine rivers. In 1848 he was in command of one of the expeditions sent to search for Franklin. He wrote the natural history notes for both of Franklin's *Narratives* and also helped compile the valuable *Fauna Boreali-Americana* and its companion *Flora Boreali-Americana*. [DCB IX]

> See Franklin
> chokecherry: 739; fireweed: 736; saskatoon: 739

*Sagard, Gabriel (*christened *Théodat)* fl 1614–36
He was a Recollet friar who came to Canada in 1623. He lived for approximately one year among the Hurons where, with two other Recollets, he built a small convent 'in the form of a garden bower.' He spent his time praying, studying the language, and visiting the families. After his recall to France in 1624 he wrote two books about his Canadian sojourn: *Le grand voyage au pays des Hurons* (Paris 1632), a remarkable study of the people and terrain, and *L'histoire du Canada* (Paris 1636).

He also compiled a useful collection of French expressions translated into Huron.   [DCB I]

> *The Long Journey To The Country of the Hurons* translated by H.H. Langton, edited by George M. Wrong. The Champlain Society, volume 25. Toronto 1939. First published France 1632
>> cardinal flower: 51; jack-in-the-pulpit: 195–6

Sarrazin, Michel 1659–1734

He was born in Burgundy and trained in medicine. He came to Canada in 1685 and was appointed surgeon-major of the colonial regular troops a year later. He returned to France in 1694 and spent three years studying medicine and learning botany from Joseph de Tournefort at the Jardin royale des plantes. In 1697 he returned to Quebec to a varied career that included significant contributions to medicine, zoology, and botany in early Canada. For many years he was a corresponding member of the Académie royale des sciences in Paris and he sent seeds and plants for the Jardin des plantes. Tournefort named one of these plants *Sarracenia purpurea* (pitcher-plant) after him. [DCB II]

Selkirk, Thomas Douglas, Earl of 1771–1820

He was born in Scotland and succeeded to the title in 1799. He was educated at Edinburgh University, where Sir Walter Scott became one of his closest friends. His attempt to found a colony for poor Highlanders and Irish on the Red River in 1802 was not permitted lest it interfere with the workings of the Hudson's Bay Company. Selkirk did obtain a grant for land in Upper Canada and Prince Edward Island in 1803 and in August of that year the first 800 settlers sailed for the Island, followed by Selkirk. He travelled extensively in the United States and Canada before returning to an active political career in Scotland in 1804. By 1811 Selkirk and his family had purchased so many shares in the Hudson's Bay Company that he was effectively in control. He was granted 45 million acres of land in the Winnipeg basin (large parts of what is now Manitoba and Minnesota), and set about founding his long-cherished colony. The Nor'westers, who disputed the Hudson's Bay Company's claims to the territory, resented this greatly. So began a tangled chain of events that led to the foundation of Winnipeg, the famous battle of Seven Oaks, and a series of raids, counter-raids, and

legal battles which depleted the resources of the North West Company and led to its union with the Hudson's Bay Company in 1821. Selkirk's health was ruined by the controversy and he died in the south of France.   [DNB; OX; MAC]

> *Lord Selkirk's Diary: 1803–1804. A Journal of His Travels In British North America* edited by Patrick C.T. White. The Champlain Society, volume 35. Toronto 1958
>> moss: 191

Simcoe, Elizabeth Posthuma (Gwillim) 1766–1850

She was born at Whitchurch in Herefordshire, the posthumous daughter of one of General Wolfe's majors of brigade. An heiress, at the age of sixteen she married John Graves Simcoe. She accompanied him to Upper Canada in 1791 when he was appointed the first lieutenant governor. She kept a fascinating journal during her years in North America. She also made many sketches of the landscape in both line and watercolour.   [OX; Harper]

> *The Diary of Mrs. John Graves Simcoe … 1792–6* edited by J. Ross Robertson. Toronto 1911. Reprinted Toronto 1973
>> balm: 176; blueberry: 237; cranberry: 161; may apple: 136; sweet flag: 274–5

Southesk, James Carnegie, Earl of 1827–1905

He was born in Edinburgh and educated there and at Sandhurst. In 1859–60 he went to Canada and travelled through some of the lesser-known sections of the West. Fifteen years later he published an account of this journey. He devoted the remainder of his life to writing poetry and to antiquarian researches.   [MAC, DNB]

> *Saskatchewan And The Rocky Mountains: A Diary and Narrative of Travel … in 1859 and 1860* Edinburgh 1875. Reprinted Edmonton 1969
>> garlic: 74; harebell: 73; saskatoon: 301–2; tiger-lily: 70

Stacey, George 1805–62

The son of an ordnance clerk in the Tower of London, he fell into bad company and incurred such large debts that his distracted father had to mortgage his own future for years. In 1836 the erring George was sent with his family to farm in Canada in order to escape prison and his low companions. He was never to return to England but spent the rest of his life as a farmer near Sherbrooke, Quebec. After great poverty, misfortune, and near starvation during the first winters, the family eventually achieved a life of comparative comfort. *The Stacey Letters* (1836–58) were discovered in a stamp sale catalogue. [*Lifelines*]

    Lifelines: The Stacey Letters 1836–1858 edited by Jane Vansittart. London 1976
      poison ivy: 75, 79

Strickland, Samuel 1804–67
He was the brother of Susanna Moodie and Catharine Parr Traill. He emigrated to Canada in 1825 and farmed near Peterborough. In 1828 John Galt hired him as an 'engineer' for the Canada Company and he helped to develop Guelph and Goderich. In 1832 he settled at Lakefield where he became a justice of the peace and captain in the militia among other activities. He also ran an agricultural school for young Englishmen. His *Twenty-Seven Years in Canada West,* while less well-known than his sisters' books, is still of considerable interest for its honest and sensible approach to the colonial experience. [DCB IX]

    Twenty-Seven Years In Canada West, or, The Experience of an Early Settler edited by Agnes Strickland. 2 Volumes in one. Edmonton 1972. First published 1853
      ash: 44–5 II; birch: 53 II; cherry: 29 II; hemlock: 231 I; plum: 171 I; raspberry: 310–11 I

Thompson, David 1770–1857
This great geographer was educated at the Grey Coat School, Westminster, and then apprenticed to the Hudson's Bay Company at the age of 14. He spent the subsequent years at various northern posts as a clerk, but often exploring and surveying. In 1797 he moved to the North West Company. He became a partner in 1804 and was occupied in explorations and fur-trading on the western plains and the Pacific coast until 1812. He was the first white man to descend the Columbia River from its source to its mouth. He named the Fraser River after Simon Fraser (who had named a river after Thompson). His map of western Canada was the basis of many later maps. He later spent ten years surveying the Canadian-American boundary for the International Boundary Commission, and ultimately died at Longueuil, Quebec, in great poverty. His *Narrative* was not published until 1916. [MAC, OX]

    Travels In Western North America, 1784–1812 edited by Victor G. Hopwood.

Toronto 1971. First published Toronto 1916, by the Champlain Society
    camass: 291; labrador tea: 140; moss: 251

Traill, Catharine Parr (Strickland) 1802–99
She was born in London, England, the sister of Susanna Moodie and Samuel Strickland. In 1832 she married Thomas Traill, a retired officer of the Royal Scots Fusiliers and emigrated with him to Upper Canada near Peterborough. Because of her serene temperament and keen interest in nature, she endured the hardships of pioneer life with more equanimity than did her sister. Her judicious accounts of the difficulties and pleasures of the emigrant's life still make enjoyable reading. Her many books include stories for children and two classic botanical works: *Canadian Wild Flowers* (1868) and *Studies in Plant Life in Canada* (1885).
[MAC; Traill *Backwoods*]

    The Backwoods of Canada: Selections edited by Clara Thomas. Toronto 1966. First published London 1836
      bloodroot: 84; fireweed: 78; hepatica: 83; lady's slipper: 87; pitcher plant: 90; rice: 68; violet: 85; wood-cress: 83
    The Canadian Settler's Guide introduction by Clara Thomas. Toronto 1969. First edition 1855. First published Toronto 1854 as *The female emigrant's guide*
      wintergreen: 228
    Canadian Wild Flowers Painted and Lithographed by Agnes Fitzgibbon with Botanical Descriptions by C.P. Traill Montreal 1868. Reprinted Toronto 1972.
      columbine: 35; trillium: 31

Verrazzano, Giovanni da c 1485–c 1528
He was born near Florence, Italy, and travelled widely in the Middle East as a young man, spending several years in Cairo as a commercial agent. After joining the maritime service of France, he sailed from Dieppe in 1523 on a voyage 'to discover new lands.' During this six-month voyage he became the first European, according to reliable accounts, to sail the coast of North America from Florida to Newfoundland. His brother Gerolamo made a map of his discoveries in 1529 (now in the Vatican) which shows the name 'Nova Gallia' (New France) for the first time. On a second trip to America in 1528, he was killed and eaten by Caribs on an island in the Lesser Antilles. His famous *Letter* contains the earliest exploratory

description of the North Atlantic coast and the earliest scientific account of the Aboriginals north of Mexico. [DCB I]

>*The Relation of John Verarzanus, a Florentine, of the lands by him discovered ... 1524* from *Divers Voyages Touching The Discovery of America* edited by J.W. Jones. Published by the Hakluyt Society, 1st series volume 7. London 1850. First published London 1582. violet: 62

Weld, Isaac 1774–1856

This young Irish painter and writer travelled widely in North America between 1795 and 1797 seeking 'an agreeable place of abode' as an escape from the turbulence of 'war and anarchy' in Europe. He enjoyed himself but remarked 'I shall leave this continent without a sigh, and without entertaining the slightest wish to revisit it.' Despite his harsh comments, his account of his *Travels*, published in 1799, became deservedly famous at once, passing through several editions and many translations. In later life he became a member of the Royal Dublin Society and a well-known topographer. [DNB]

>*Travels Through The States of North America And The Provinces Of Upper and Lower Canada: 1795, 1796 & 1797* 2 volumes. 4th edition London 1807. First published London 1799
>>birch: 17 II; plum: 37–8 II; sumac: 319–20 II; tobacco: 28 II

White, Catharine (Crysdale) 1782?–1863?

Her parents came from England to settle on a farm in the United States. Later, as ardent Loyalists, they moved first to Sorel and then to Sidney, near Belleville, where they were granted 800 acres of land. She married Josiah White in 1812 and moved to Cobourg in 1813, then 'quite a Wilderness' with a few small clearings, three houses, and a corduroy road to the lake. Her interesting observations are included in Talman's *Loyalist Narratives from Upper Canada*.

>*Loyalist Narratives From Upper Canada* edited by J.J. Talman. The Champlain Society, volume 27. Toronto 1946
>>maple: 353

BIBLIOGRAPHY

GENERAL

Fredi Chiapelli (editor) *First Images of America: The Impact of the New World on the Old* Berkeley 1976

Alice M. Coats *The Plant Hunters* New York 1970. First published as *The Quest for Plants* 1968 (Coats)

– *The Treasury of Flowers* London 1975

Dictionary of American Biography (DAB)

Dictionary of Canadian Biography (DCB; information not yet published but available through the offices of the DCB is identified as DCB file)

Dictionary of National Biography (DNB)

Gerald M. Craig *Early Travellers in the Canadas: 1791–1867* Toronto 1955 (Craig)

Pamela Dixon *Ginseng* London 1976

Charlotte Erichsen-Brown *Use of Plants for the Past 500 Years* Aurora Ontario 1979

Merritt Lyndon Fernald and Alfred Charles Kinsey *Edible Plants of Eastern North America* Cornwall-on-Hudson NY 1943

Richard Gorer *The Growth of Gardens* London and Boston 1978

J. Russell Harper *Early Painters and Engravers in Canada* Toronto 1970 (Harper)

Ann Leighton *Early American Gardens* Boston 1970

Norah Story *The Oxford Companion to Canadian History and Literature* Toronto 1967;

William Toye (editor) *Supplement to the Oxford Companion to Canadian History and Literature* Toronto 1973 (OX)

Reuben Gold Thwaites (editor) *The Jesuit Relations and Allied Documents: Travels and Explorations of the Jesuit Missionaries in New France, 1610–1791* 73 volumes; Cleveland 1896–1901

H.M. Tory (editor) *A History of Science in Canada* Toronto 1939 (Tory)

W. Stewart Wallace (editor) *The Macmillan Dictionary of Canadian Biography* 3rd edition Toronto 1963 (MAC)

J.R. Anderson *Trees and Shrubs, Food, Medicinal and Poisonous Plants of British Columbia* Victoria 1925

Nathaniel, Lord Britton, and the Hon. Addison Brown *An Illustrated Flora of the Northern United States and Canada 2nd edition* New York 1970. First published 1913

A.C. Budd *Wild Plants of the Canadian Prairies* Ottawa 1957

Lewis J. Clark *Wild Flowers of British Columbia* Sidney BC 1973

R.G.H. Cormack *Wild Flowers of Alberta* Edmonton 1967

Clarence Frankton and Gerald A. Mulligan *Weeds of Canada* 2nd edition Ottawa 1970. First published 1955

R.C. Hosie *Native Trees of Canada* 8th edition Toronto 1979

Frère Marie-Victorin *Flore laurentienne* Montréal 1964. First published 1935

F.H. Montgomery *Native Wild Plants of Eastern Canada and the Adjacent Northeastern United States* Toronto 1962

Morin, N. (ed.) *Flora of North America*. Oxford University Press. New York Volumes 1-3. 1993

Oliver Perry Medsger *Edible Wild Plants* New York and London 1972

Gerald A. Mulligan *Common Weeds of Canada* Toronto 1976

Newmaster , S.G. , A. Lehela, P.W.C. Uhlig, S. McMurray and M.J. Oldham *Ontario Plant List 1998*. Ontario Forest Research Institute. Sault Ste. Marie.

Roger Tory Peterson and Margaret McKenny *A Field Guide to Wildflowers of Northeastern and Northcentral North America* Boston 1968

Chester A. Reed *Flower Guide: Wildflowers East of the Rockies* New York 1920

P.A. Rydberg *Flora of the Rocky Mountains and Adjacent Plains* New York 1917

H.J. Scoggan *The Flora of Canada* 4 volumes; Ottawa 1978

– *Flora of Manitoba* Ottawa 1957

Nancy J. Turner and Adam F. Szczawinski *Edible Wild Plants of Canada* 4 volumes; Ottawa 1978–80

F.R. Vance, J.R. Jowsey, and J.S. McLean *Wildflowers across the Prairies* Saskatoon 1977

Mary Alice Downie is the author of many books for both adults and children, including *The Well-Filled Cupboard*, *Bright Paddles*, *The Wind Has Wings*, *Honor Bound*, and *Danger in Disguise*. She lives in Kingston, Ontario.

Mary Hamilton has written poetry, articles and several books, including *The Tin-Lined Trunk*, *The Sky Caribou*, *A New World Bestiary* and *Wild Edibles*. She lives in Kingston, Ontario.

E.J. Revell began painting flowers in 1968 at his summer home near Coldwater, Ontario. His work now hangs in many private collections. He is Professor Emeritus of the Department of Near and Middle Eastern Civilization at the University of Toronto. He currently resides in Oxfordshire, England.

Adéle Crowder, Technical Consultant, is Professor Emeritus of the Department of Biology, Queen's University.